Stuck No More

PRACTICAL SELF-COACHING FOR EVERYDAY PROBLEMS

Lisa C. Gregory

Dr. Steve Jeffs

IngramSpark

U.S.A

Copyright © 2024 Lisa C Gregory and Steve Jeffs

All rights reserved. No part of this publication may be reproduced, distributed, or transmitted in any form or by any means, including photocopying, recording, or other electronic or mechanical methods, without the prior written permission of the authors, except in the case of brief quotations embodied in critical reviews and certain other noncommercial uses permitted by copyright law. For permission requests, write to the authors at info@stucknomorebook.com

Published in the United States by Lisa C Gregory and Dr. Steve Jeffs.

Book cover design by Katarina Naskovski. Illustrations by Hamza Abubakar. Book Layout ©2017 BookDesignTemplates.com. Image Copyrights: CartoonStock Image Chapter 2: The Power of Purpose. Wikipedia Chapter 4: Yerkes-Dodson Law

www.StuckNoMoreBook.com

Ordering Information:

Quantity sales. Special discounts are available on quantity purchases by corporations, associations, and others. For details, contact the group sales team at info@stucknomorebook.com

Stuck No More: Practical Self-Coaching for Everyday Problems/ Lisa C. Gregory and Dr. Steve Jeffs. —1st ed.

Testimonials

"**A phenomenal book on how to overcome challenges -** both in your career and in life. Using easy to follow examples and language, Lisa and Steve have created a highly readable and thought-provoking guide on how to overcome the challenges that have you stuck with seemingly no way out. I highly recommend this book for those who want to improve careers as well as individual lives." – Guy Burnett, PhD in Public Law and American Government, United States

"**A wonderful self-coaching guide that anyone can access and use.** The tools are so impactful while at the same time they are described in such a user-friendly way. I cannot recommend this book enough. It is truly a tool that I will be sharing with others." - Lissa Qualls, MCC (Master Certified Coach), ClarityOk, United States

"**A commonsense approach.** I enjoyed seeing concepts illustrated in a way that makes them easier to apply, thinking logically how things affect each other, and feeling like I can get unstuck from my own ruts. Thank you, Lisa and Steve." - Suzy Andersen, Certified Life Coach, United States

"**Overcome personal obstacles.** This book is a must read for anyone looking to take control of their life. It's clear, step-by-step format and real-life examples will help you unlock new perspectives and solutions."
– Hagar El Battouty, Chief Transformation Officer, Egypt

Contents

Why Learn to Self-Coach? 1

I Should, But I Don't 13

I've Tried Everything 37

The Pressure is Too Much 69

Listen to Me! 93

What to Do Next 117

Additional Resources 121

Dedication

This book is dedicated to all the smart, well-meaning, capable people who, like us, get stuck and just need a little nudge to find their own answers and way forward.

Acknowledgements

Lisa C Gregory

First, I must thank you, Steve. You proposed this project so we could stay in touch over the years and what an amazing project it has been! Thank you to my mother, Arlene Chapman, who was lovingly relentless in asking for updates on the book and to both my parents who are my first coaches and best teachers. Thank you to my amazing husband, confidant, and best friend, Joe. Your belief in me and joy in my success gives me courage. Thank you to my coach Lissa Qualls who asked, "why not publish now?", and to Sara Price for editing and offering feedback. And finally, thank you to all my clients, friends and family members who have shared your hearts and stories with me, been open to my many questions, and taught me how to be a friend, confidant, counselor, and coach.

Dr. Steve Jeffs

Immense thanks to Lisa, my co-author, for her drive and dedication that brought this book to life. To my beloved family—Rebecca, and my children, Amelia, Nikita, and Leila—your unwavering support is my greatest treasure. I'm grateful to my clients, whose narratives have not only influenced this work but also my own journey. A special acknowledgement to DeAnna Murphy and the Thrivin team, whose passion for transformative growth has been both an inspiration and a testament to the power of our collective efforts. And to my friends and colleagues, your silent contributions have left an indelible mark on every chapter of this book. Each of you has, in your unique way, helped to shape the story that I am honored to tell.

CHAPTER 1

Why Learn to Self-Coach?

"A good coach can change a game. A great coach can change a life." - John Wooden

"What if you were the coach and the life that changed was your own?" - Lisa C Gregory and Dr. Steve Jeffs

A coach has an interesting role and perspective. In any sport, the coach stands off the field, court, or platform. From that vantage point, the coach can see the big picture, potential problems, and solutions. They can do all this without the worry of getting pummeled by the opponent coming down the court or field. Coaches have space, safety, and perspective that the players on the field don't have. If you are on the field, you can't take a step back or get a different perspective. If you do, you'll get hit - hard!

We want to teach you how to safely step off the field for a moment, create some space and perspective so you can see the big picture, see potential problems, and solutions to the situations in your life. We want to teach you to be your own coach.

Why Learn to Self-Coach?

Everyone needs a coach - a trusted advisor who can see the field you are on, see your skills and the challenges facing you, and work with you to create success. Most often that coach is external, however that coach can be you and we will teach you how.

Why is a coach so helpful? Like we said, when you are on the field it can be easy to lose sight of the big picture and the solutions to your challenges. A coach asks good questions that will lift your view, helps you see things you didn't see before, and helps you find your own solutions.

Why don't we all have a coach? There are several reasons. One of the main reasons is a lack of access. Do you know a professional coach, a really good one? Can you afford to pay for their time?

Another challenge is being able to find the right coach. Then, once you find them, how do you get a hold of them when you need them the most? Are they available when things melt down, blow up, or fall apart?

What if you could coach yourself?

You can! We are going to teach you how through the resources, questions, and examples in this book. This book is about getting you unstuck - right now while the game is still in play. Reading the chapters and using the questions in them is like pausing the game, calling a timeout, and taking a coach's view. Doing so will help you get unstuck so you can re-enter the game with better options to get better results.

This book is not about asking general coaching questions at a high level. It's about getting practical, applicable actions to help you become "Stuck No More". It's about helping you learn to coach yourself using questions that we as professional coaches use over and over to help our clients get results.

Why are we sharing our best coaching questions?

Because we can't coach everyone! In our own coaching practices, our goal is to help our clients practice coaching themselves so they can step off the field during the game and coach themselves into better solutions. We want them to be able to hear our questions in their heads as they tackle the situations, tasks, and relationships in their lives wherever or whenever they feel stuck. They hear our questions over and over until they become their own questions, in their own voice…until they become their own coach.

We are grateful to the thousands of clients who have let us help them through everyday problems. Their experiences led to this book. If you are willing to read and apply the tools here, we will be able to also help you become your own coach and get yourself unstuck from the everyday problems that you face!

Whether you are an employee, business owner, leader, parent, volunteer, retiree, or student…if you are human, you can become your own coach and get unstuck. Asking and answering the right questions at the right time can help you get unstuck from the situations, relationships, and tasks where you feel confused, blind, or uncertain. It happens to all of us, and a well-placed question from another perspective can help us get unstuck.

Here is an example that almost everyone can relate to:

> Remember the time when you were looking for your glasses (sunglasses, reading glasses, eyeglasses) and couldn't find them anywhere? You searched and searched, knowing that they had to be nearby! You just used them!
>
> Finally, in exasperation you went to someone else in your household and pleaded, "have you seen my glasses? I can't find them anywhere!". To which they, with a different perspective, asked you a

simple question. "Have you checked the top of your head?"

And there you found them. Perched on the top of your head, right where you put them.

The answer was obvious when you knew where to look.

This is a simple story but it's an example of being so stuck that you can't see other potential solutions until someone from outside the situation shows you where to look.

That is what having a coach is all about. Having someone you can speak to who has a different perspective than your own. Their questions are often simple, and obvious (like the glasses on your head), yet their power lies in their outside view, helping you to get unstuck. You won't always have a coach available to talk to. That's why we wrote this book. It's an "on demand, just in time, there when you need it resource."

It's a tool. Stuck No More is filled with questions that will help you find your own new perspectives to help you see differently and get unstuck. These questions and the space they provide allow insights to come to you so you can solve your own problems. We will provide the questions. You will provide the space to explore your answers to the questions.

When you get stuck, open the book.

We are inside, ready to ask you questions and invite you to create space to hear your own answers. We are here like coaches in your pocket - there when you need us - to ask thought-provoking questions that will help you get unstuck.

Now, here's what you WON'T find in this book.

- You won't find an answer to every question that troubles you.

- You won't find elaborate theoretical explanations.
- You won't find complex models and maps that are difficult to remember and use.
- You won't find fluffy feel-good ideas that don't actually work in the real world.
- And you won't find partial answers that entice you to buy another book or purchase an online course so you can get the full answer.

This is an on demand, just in time, there when you need it resource, so You WILL have the top questions we use to get people unstuck 80% of the time.

You will find insights and tools in each chapter of the book that will help you get unstuck and create more success in your life with the pressing questions you have. You will fight the current fires in your life. Later, you can do fire prevention and fire management. For now, you will get unstuck and moving again in the situations that are causing you the most frustration in your life.

The focus of this book is NOW. What you need NOW. It is not a reflection on your past experiences and it's not even future focused. It is simply focused on where you are stuck now and what you need to do today to get unstuck. It's true that by applying what you learn here you will become more self-aware and prepared for the future. However, the impact on your future is a side benefit. The primary focus is the challenges facing you today, the match you are currently playing, the mud you are currently stuck in.

There are a couple of ways to use this book.

1) If you are currently struggling and stuck with something, if the fire is raging now, then you can jump to a chapter that sounds promising and start there.

2) If you are currently doing okay but know you will get stuck again at some point (like we all do), then you can read it from cover to cover and learn all the strategies. That's like adding more tools to your firefighting toolkit.

3) If you are a reader of self-help and self-improvement books, then read or skim each chapter and then, come back to the book when you get stuck. You can re-read sections and use the questions and examples to find your solutions.

Regardless of where you start, you'll find a common structure in each chapter.

Each chapter will introduce you to a specific tool. The tool will help you step off the field and answer a series of powerful questions that will lead you to better solutions, new perspectives, and get you unstuck.

To make it easy for you, each chapter is organized into the following sections:

1) **How do I know when to use this tool?** We share the thoughts and emotions people feel when they are stuck in a place where this strategy or tool is really helpful to use. You'll be able to answer the question, "Is this the tool I need for my situation right now?"

2) **What is the tool?** Now that you know that this tool can help you with the situation you have in mind, we unveil the tool itself. We share with you the handful of powerful coaching questions you can use to get yourself unstuck.

3) **What does this tool really mean and how/why does it work?** We give you the back story and pull back the covers on your core problem. We help you see what is really going on, why you are really stuck and share some insights as to why and how

this tool works! The coaching questions in the tool can feel like they work magic, but they aren't magic. There is a reason they work, and we share that reason with you. You'll explore some ideas and simple models. Models are helpful because they are designed specifically to guide you from where you are to where you want to be. And you can use them again and again.

4) **Can you give me an example?** YES! We will always give you an application story that highlights the mindset of the person, what was really going on, how they used and answered the coaching questions and the result or impact. Most of us learn from stories and seeing how things work. So, we've added that for you.

More application stories can be found in our Facebook group, "Stuck No More People", so check that out too. In fact, join right now so you can explore these tools with us and others.

We have also added accompanying resources online for you at www.StuckNoMoreBook.com/Resources. URLs are at the end of each chapter. This resource further explains each tool.

You can also download discussion questions to use with others if you read this book as part of a team effort, as a family or in a book/discussion club. Use the QR Code below to go to *www.StuckNoMoreBook.com/Discussion*.

Your first time through, don't just read the questions listed at the start of each chapter and think this is enough. That would be like us handing you an axe and letting you run without showing you how to use it safely and effectively. Reading about when and how to use the tool and how it works is like your safety briefing - you don't need it each time, but you do need it at least one time!

Reading about each tool also gives your brain a "heads-up" and starts to prepare your thinking to use the tool. We have heard examples of people remembering the tool, right when they needed it, after having read the chapter only once. Why not prepare your brain now to recall what you'll need later?

If you are ready to get started, jump to the start of the next chapter and let's get going!

If you want a little more context around how we are uniquely qualified to write this book before you listen to us, then read on.

We (Steve and Lisa) have worked together for over a decade. Our families and spouses are friends, we've spent time in each other's homes, vacationing, and we've built dozens of programs together. We've built and co-facilitated successful coaching-certification programs, online learning, and in-person courses together - all focused on helping people and teams decrease the toxicity they feel in their lives and work, and increase their success, energy, and results.

We come at things from very different perspectives, strengths, weaknesses, and approaches. We cover quite a spectrum of experiences and skills. These differences create some great outcomes because we are totally aligned on helping people with real, practical, applicable solutions.

Lisa Chapman Gregory

Lisa Chapman Gregory is a certified strengths coach, has earned a Masters of Instructional Technology degree, and as she likes to say, she is "a doer of the word, not a hearer only." An owner of multiple small businesses with her husband Joe, Lisa has also worked and led others in companies of all sizes.

Like you, Lisa has lots of complex situations and relationships to navigate. As a wife, stepmother, sister, sister-in-law, daughter, daughter-in-law, direct manager, employee, coach, entrepreneur, church member and community contributor, she has daily opportunities to coach herself and others. Through it all, she loves to make ideas practical and tactical.

Her two favorite questions to ask herself and others are, "...therefore, what?" (i.e. so how does that impact what I/we/you do?) and "What's important about that?" (Purpose is powerful). As a coach, Lisa is as kind as she is powerful. And she believes that being kind means telling the truth even when it is hard to hear. She's the type of friend and thought partner you want in your life if you desire change and answers.

A native of Northern Virginia in the United States, Lisa has lived in Boston, Jerusalem, Tokyo, New York City, Atlanta, and Washington DC. She and her husband now reside just outside Washington DC.

Dr. Steve Jeffs

Steve is a Master Coach, Business Psychologist and Entrepreneur. He is passionate about understanding how people can be at their best in work and in life. He earned his Doctorate in Leadership, is a deep thinker and always has more ideas he is mulling over than he can implement in a lifetime. As a coach, Steve works with senior organizational leaders, trains coaches with the Coactive Training Institute, and is the Director of Coaching with TheCoachingToolsCompany.com

With a background in leadership development, Steve came to coaching because he saw that people were learning how to be better, but not implementing these ideas. They were stuck - stuck in expectations of how they saw themselves, and stuck in a need to look competent, capable and successful. Steve saw that unless it was safe to change, people would choose to stay stuck. If they could hide their weaknesses from others, they would, even if it meant frustration and pain for themselves and others. He now helps people change that for themselves through coaching.

Steve has had a diverse career with roles in the Military, as a consultant, coach, entrepreneur, executive and investor. As an Australian, he works globally and has lived in Thailand, UAE and is now living outside London in the UK with his wonderful wife and three brilliant daughters.

As a hobby, Steve loves extreme and technical SCUBA diving. He is inspired by the freedom, opportunity to explore, and the ability to enter a completely different world. More than this, SCUBA diving is based upon your readiness to save yourself. All the training is about giving you the knowledge to recognize what might happen, and to have the skills and tools to prevent, and recover. Just like diving, this book will help you to STOP, BREATHE and THINK, allowing you to be Stuck No More.

Our Voices

Both of us (Lisa and Steve) read and reviewed all parts of this book (many, many times). We took turns taking the lead on the writing of certain sections and through the editing process we blended our voices together. You'll hear both our perspectives and "voices" throughout the book.

For clarity, where we share personal stories, we label them, so you know who is talking. Otherwise, this book is from us to you. When you are done with it, you will be Stuck No More. You'll be free from 80% of the everyday problems that drain your energy, reduce your success, and frustrate you. You'll use practical self-coaching to step back from the field, see the big picture, find better solutions and be more confident jumping back into the game!

Let's get to it!

CHAPTER 2

I Should, But I Don't

"Life is never made unbearable by circumstances, but only by lack of meaning and purpose." – Viktor Frankl

"I should do it, but I don't want to, so I don't."

How do you overcome procrastination and do the stuff you don't want to do. Defining your purpose will help you to work through tasks and relationships that you are avoiding.

If you are thinking...

- "I really don't want to do this, but I feel like I should."
- "Why don't I just get it done?"
- "I really don't want to deal with him on Monday, but I have to face him."
- "I don't even want to talk to her, but I feel like I can't just ignore her."

Or if you are feeling…

- Trapped
- Stuck

- A sense of dread
- Avoidance, or
- A general reluctance toward something or someone…

Then, **Using the Power of Purpose** tool will help you to…

- get motivated.
- take in a wider view.
- see new pathways forward.

Using the Power of Purpose helps you get beyond the "I don't want to do this but feel I should do it" phase and quickly move to "I just did it!" or "I'm choosing not to do it."

When you need to do something that is not **motivating** in itself, defining your Purpose helps move you to action. It will help you either take action or let go of your own expectation that you must do it and just not do it. This tool is powerful for difficult tasks and relationships because it helps you identify 'WHY' you want to get it done and see more ways to actually do it or let it go. Using the Power of Purpose tool gets you out of the no man's land of wanting something done but not wanting to do it.

What Are the Self-Coaching Questions to Help You Get Unstuck?

Using the Power of Purpose:

1) What happens if I don't do it? (Is not doing the thing an option? Why or why not?)
2) What do I really want in this situation?
3) What is important about what I really want?
4) What actions are in my control?
5) What might it look like/feel like if I'm successful?

What Does This Tool Really Mean and How/Why Does it Work?

To understand this tool and how it works, let's first define purpose for the focus of getting you unstuck.

What is Purpose?

Purpose is the reason something is done or created, or the reason something exists. It refers to the sense of direction or intention behind actions, decisions, or life choices.

Using the Power of Purpose is a simple, yet powerful tool to help you get unstuck.

Using the Power of Purpose invites you to get clear on your "Why". When you know 'why' you want to do something, then the 'what to do', and 'how to do it' become easier and much clearer. This chapter is all about helping you to use the Power of Purpose to get unstuck, get motivated, and get moving.

When we are talking about Purpose, we need to be very clear about what type of Purpose we are thinking about. There are many different levels of Purpose. These can range from the highest level of existential questions such as "why am I alive?" and "why am I on this planet?" and go all the way down to "why do I like ice cream?".

We are not talking about destiny or life Purpose here. There are many books, programs and coaches that explore your life's purpose and help you define the meaning of your life. These can be very helpful, but that high level of purpose is beyond the focus of this chapter and book.

This chapter focuses on finding your Purpose in a particular situation or relationship where you are feeling stuck, where you are procrastinating, or are otherwise not moving forward. It will help you to clarify your Purpose "in the moment" when you are facing immediate challenges related to people or things you feel you need to do. Together, we will dive into these "now" Purposes to give you clear steps that will get you moving when things are difficult.

It is important to remember that Purpose Definition is not defining **HOW** you are going to get to your target. It is also not **WHAT** you are going to do. Defining your Purpose is larger than **HOW** and **WHAT.** It answers the bigger question of, "**WHY** am I doing this?" or, in more practical terms, "What outcome do I really want in this situation, conversation, work, project, choice, relationship, etc.?" AND "What is important about that outcome?"

Defining your Purpose involves getting really clear on what you want and why. It is about identifying the ultimate target you want to hit in <u>this</u> situation, for <u>this</u> task, in <u>this</u> relationship, or in <u>this</u> conversation.

Stuck Thinking

Unstuck Thinking

The figures above show that the difference between stuck thinking and unstuck thinking is one simple step, clarifying "Why am I doing this?". Unfortunately, it is also an easy step to forget, especially when you are frustrated that you are not making enough progress. In other words, when you are stuck.

In this model, the **Now** represents the moment you are facing a problem or challenges. In Stuck Thinking, this problem needs addressing, and it needs addressing **Now**! So, you ask yourself "**What** do I do?" You look for ways to solve the problem. As soon as you think of one idea or an easy solution, you quickly move to the next step and ask, "**How** do I do it? **How** do I take steps to solve my problem?" Notice there is no arrow at the end of that "**How**" in the diagram above. When you are in Stuck Thinking, the **How** doesn't fix your problem and you get stuck pushing on the one idea, the one solution you thought of. When it doesn't seem to work, you just push harder

In Unstuck Thinking the additional step of "Why Am I Doing This" changes how things work. The **Now** is still the problem you are facing. The problem still feels urgent and you believe it needs to be solved, yet Unstuck Thinking reminds you to take a moment to step back and answer some key questions rather than jumping to a solution.

One question is, "Is this really a problem that needs to be solved **Now**?"

Ask yourself, "What happens if I don't solve it?" Not solving the problem is always an option – even if is an option you don't want to take. Pause and consider what would happen if you didn't solve this now. Not why you 'should' solve it, but what are the actual consequences if it is not solved. Is not taking action a viable option? Why or why not?

In many cases, you don't want the consequences that will come if you don't do the thing, so you feel pressured to do it. But recognizing that you actually have a choice to not do something is important. And sometimes the answer really is to not take action, or that now is not the time to do anything at all.

But sometimes, the only person pressuring yourself to get something done right now is you. Sometimes the answer is, "no, it doesn't have to be solved at all". For example, do you have to find your son's soccer cleats/boots? Maybe the answer is no. Does it really need to be you? Perhaps your son could look for them. Or someone else?

If you do choose to take action, then consider for a moment **WHY** you want to take action. This is more than just "because I want to avoid the consequences of doing nothing".

Now you need a real reason WHY you WANT to DO it? WHY does this problem need solving and solving now?

Connecting with your **Why** helps you clearly see the importance of solving the problem. This knowledge helps you to identify and prioritize **What** you can do to achieve your **Why**. You'll see multiple options and identify additional ideas about what you could do. You can then compare those options and ideas to your **Why** and choose the best **How** to get unstuck.

And, if it doesn't work, you'll use the arrow at the end of the diagram to come back to a different **What Do I Do** and **How Do I Do It** and keep trying different ideas until you are successful. By connecting to **Why**, you don't get stuck in a limited **What** or **How**.

Identifying your **Why**, your purpose, makes all the difference!

So, if you find yourself feeling stuck and jumping to a **What Do I Do** and **How Do I Do It** that aren't working, remember to lift your gaze. Ask yourself the larger questions of **Why** to uncover your purpose. It's not just about finding a way out of the situation; it's about knowing which way is worth going.

Something to Think About

As Alice in Wonderland learned from the Cheshire Cat, without knowing your end goal, your Why, then any path will do.

Alice: I was just wondering if you could help me find my way.

Cheshire Cat: Well, that depends on where you want to get to.

Alice: Oh, it really doesn't matter, as long as...

Cheshire Cat: Then it really doesn't matter which way you go.

Defining your Why will help you then choose the best What Do I Do and How Do I Do It for getting there.

When Do I Use the Power of Purpose?

Use the Power of Purpose whenever your path forward is not clear to you, or if you think the path is clear but you are just not moving forward.

If you don't know why you are doing something or find yourself procrastinating on doing (or trying to do) something that you don't want to, then clarify your Purpose.

You might think about it like this…

Imagine yourself at the bottom of a huge hill that you have decided you MUST climb. For many reasons you have decided you HAVE TO do this. It is going to take you more than an hour to climb up, and it will be more than an hour of sweat, pain, and effort.

Imagine how your legs are going to feel as you go. They will be sore, they will feel weak, and you will need to rest. Climbing this hill is going to be exhausting, and difficult, and you just don't want to do it. Just looking at this enormous hill you feel drained and begin dreading the hike.

This is how it feels when you don't have a clear Purpose. And it doesn't only happen when you have to climb physical hills. It shows up whenever you face a metaphorical "hill" in your life that you need to get over.

Think back on some of the "hills" in your life where having a Purpose may have helped you see things differently, feel differently and move forward differently.

Maybe it was before a wedding or reunion when you found out that a person you have a tough relationship with was going to be there. You immediately felt distressed just thinking about seeing that person and the uncomfortable conversations that would happen.

Perhaps it wasn't a wedding, but it was (or is) the pit that forms in your stomach each Sunday night as you think about the Monday morning team call you need to attend, "knowing" that "That Person" will be there. You just know that they will say some snarky, or aggravating comments just to annoy you.

Or perhaps it is a task that needs to get done. You know the one. It's the one you put off by first cleaning your office, filing paperwork, or dusting your shelves. In fact, this is the task that motivates you to do absolutely ANYTHING to avoid doing it.

All of these examples have something in common. In each of them, there is something that you've decided you must do, but you don't want to. So, you procrastinate.

There are lots of reasons you procrastinate, but many times there is an emotional barrier you feel when you just THINK about doing that thing or talking to that person. You think, "I've got to do this thing, but it's hard and all I'm doing is thinking about it. I haven't even started yet!"

Which makes it even harder to start because, if just thinking about it is this hard, what is it going to be like when you actually have to do the thing you are dreading?!

When you find yourself in this place, your thinking has narrowed right down to focus only on the challenge and difficulties you face (or imagine facing). You get stuck, and all you can see is the pain, conflict or judgment of other people. You focus on avoiding mistakes, or on trying not to fail. And this narrow focus hurts!

> **Steve**: A real example of a stuck focus comes from my daughter's experience with Type-1 Diabetes. She was recently diagnosed, and it's been quite an adjustment for her to go through multiple injections every day. Many people go through their lives avoiding needles at all costs, and here was a 10-year-old having to give herself 5-7 injections every

> single day - knowing that she would also have to do this for the rest of her life!
>
> I remember, one day, her mother and I sat down with her to do an injection at around 6pm. On this day, the injection was absolutely something that she did not want to do. Her dread of the injection made it even worse. She tried everything to avoid the injection. She went to the bathroom, she checked the expiry date on the insulin, she started conversations to distract us. Whenever we pressed her to take action, she would tell us things like "Just wait!" "I'll do it" and "I'm not ready yet."
>
> I was stuck. If she had to give permission for the injection to happen, I could think of nothing more to do. I had done everything she asked, given space, given time, answered questions, yet she was not progressing. All I could think of was to hold her down and force the injection into her. I didn't want to do this, but the injection needed to happen and the longer it took, the higher her blood sugar would go, and the worse it would be.
>
> The conversation repeated and continued along the lines of "It hurts. I don't want it to hurt. What if it hurts? I don't want it to hurt…"
>
> There were tears, emotions, difficulty, upset, all the while her Mum and I were trying everything we could to help her move forward. 45 minutes later, we were still going. No progress - we had still not even started up the hill.

As you can see in this story, everyone was stuck. Everyone became narrowly focused on things that did not help.

How Does Using the Power of Purpose Help?

As demonstrated in the story, when you are triggered, your focus narrows. When your focus narrows, it's like putting blinders on. Blinders help horses focus on running the track before them. It works well with horses, but not people.

When you put blinders on, all you can see is the next solution that occurs to you. And because the situation is stressful, your vision of the situation reduces down until you can only see what is directly in front of you, the things you dread. All you can see is the next step. Because of the blinders, you never get to ask if this is even the right path.

All Steve's daughter could see was the pain that would come as she stuck the needle into her leg. No wonder it was difficult. Sticking a needle into your leg hurts. Pushing the needle through your skin and into your leg can leave painful bruises that last for days. It makes sense that she did not want to do it.

Narrowing her focus meant that she forgot about WHY she was doing it. By focusing on the injection, she forgot what was important about the injection - her health. She forgot purpose. And that made the situation dreadful. Literally, full of dread!

>**Steve**: While my daughter was clearly stuck, so was I. All I could see was that she needed the injection. To me, it was a simple set of actions that we could have done in less than 30 seconds. The steps were

clear, the actions understood. All I needed was her permission. All she had to do was stop resisting.

As you can see, my focus was narrowed. While I was clear on why the insulin was needed, I had lost sight of the relevance of my daughter's why. I expected the logic of "high sugars = insulin correction", and that "we just have to do it" would be enough to get it done.

When you are stuck like this, it is important to bring your attention back to Purpose. As you shift your awareness to your Purpose, you place your focus squarely on where you want to go. As you focus on where you want to go, you can begin to connect with why you are doing something. As you do this, it becomes easier to do these things that you don't want to do.

Using the Power of Purpose helps you take the blinders off. It gives you a wider view, where you not only increase your motivation, but you can also start to see new pathways to get to your destination.

Refocusing on your Purpose for doing something allows you to explore the question:

"How do I do the things I don't want to do,

           to get the things I do want to have?"

or even more powerfully:

"What is important enough to motivate me

           to get the things I do want to have?"

Steve: So, coming back to this experience with my daughter…

Having to take over an hour for each injection was not a viable, or sustainable solution for anyone. We had to think of a different approach.

As my wife and I began to think about purpose, we realized that as long as our daughter focused on the pain, she would do everything she could to avoid and delay the injections. We had to help her find a purpose that would support positive action. Together, we created and agreed on a strategy where she could earn points for doing the injections well, and that these points would entitle her to a prize of her choosing.

By setting target levels for each prize, she found a Why that was bigger than her fear of pain, and which motivated her to track and monitor her diabetes in a way that was both good for her health, and effective at gaining great prizes. She recognized that by quickly doing her insulin injections she would gain points towards a doll she really wanted. Getting the doll became much more exciting than doing the injection. Now, she had a reason to get it done quickly and practically.

More than this, not only did she get it done, but because she had a compelling 'Why', she also experienced less physical and emotional pain. To be honest, so did her mother and I.

As we can see, when Steve's daughter focused on the cost, she was thinking about the pain and bruises. And when this was her focus, there was no way that she would do the injection. Even thinking about the pain was painful.

We can also see that as Steve focused on the action, all he was thinking about was that it was not working, so he pushed harder, putting even more pressure on his fearful daughter. Unsurprisingly, as Steve pushed harder, his daughter pushed back even harder!

Yet when Steve and his wife took a moment to step back, they were able to create a meaningful purpose to support the injections and saw a new way to help their daughter connect to her own purpose. While she cannot control the pain, she can control where she focuses her attention.

As Steve took off his blinders, he was able to let go of his attachment to what he thought was important, things like efficiently getting the injection done, or doing the right thing for her health.

As he let go of what was right in front of him, Steve could consider what was important to his daughter - being successful and earning an exciting doll. By connecting with Why, everyone was able to work together in ways that were more effective and much less frustrating for everyone involved.

You have your own examples like this. Situations where you had to stop and choose to take the blinders off so that you could see the bigger picture. Maybe you still didn't want to take the action, but achieving the outcome was more motivating than avoiding the pain, so you did it. It's a critical life skill and you already do it in many areas of your life. However, we all have those places where it is still

REALLY hard to widen the focus and get motivated to do a hard or dreaded thing.

It's in those areas of life, for those obstacles, for all of those hills to climb, that defining your purpose can make a huge difference. Using the Power of Purpose can get you out of the rut and back on the road again.

When you are stuck, take a step back, emotionally and mentally from the situation. Pause and focus on answering "why". By shifting your focus away from what stresses you, you reduce your own emotional intensity. You decrease your fear and worry. In essence, looking at purpose creates space between the situation you are facing and yourself so that you can make better, more effective choices.

This emotional distance is powerful because it gives you time to identify what is most important to you in a situation. Taking a step back really helps you to see something different.

Seeking purpose gives you the emotional **space** to look for what is important, AND helps you **identify** it. One action - two benefits.

A Word of Caution – The Purpose Is Not The HOW

Just a word of caution as you practice defining purpose. You must remember that purpose isn't the **How**, it's the **Why**!

When Steve focused on giving his daughter the injection, he put blinders on and was only focused on the **How**.

"How can I get this injection done?"

That's how he got stuck.

When he took the blinders off and looked at the larger **Why**

"Why might she want to get the injection done?"

then the **How** became easy, and they were no longer stuck.

If you find yourself starting at a **How** - OR you find that the first **Why** (purpose) you thought of is not getting you unstuck, then look for a bigger **Why**.

So, how do you find and define the purpose and ensure you are staying focused on the big picture **Why**, not the **How**? The answer lies in asking and answering specific questions of yourself and doing so honestly.

> **Something to Think About**
>
> In defining your **Why**, you may ask yourself **What** questions, but they aren't the **What Do I Do** questions. These **What** questions are: What is important? What do I want? and so on…When defining your purpose, you'll use these bigger picture **What** questions and they will lead you to the right **What Do I Do** answers.
>
> Like Alice in Wonderland, if you don't know What you want or Where you want to go (your purpose), you'll never get to a meaningful answer to What Do I Do or Which Way Do I Go.

So, How Do I Use the Power of Purpose?

So far, we have been exploring Why we would want to define our purpose – to get unstuck and have clear next steps. Now that we are clear on Why, we can look at How.

The How is to honestly and thoroughly answer five big picture What questions.

Using the Power of Purpose:

1) What happens if I don't do it? (Is not doing the thing an option? Why or why not?)

2) What do I really want in this situation?

3) What is important about that purpose?
4) What actions are in my control?
5) What might it look like/feel like if I'm successful?

Question 1: What happens if I don't do it? (Is not doing the thing an option? Why or why not?)

Before you start to define your purpose for a situation or relationship, first pause and just make sure you actually need to take action. What will happen if you don't do anything?

Usually, the thought of not taking action is unacceptable to us so we feel driven to do something. But sometimes, we imagine potential consequences (good or bad) that actually won't come true. It's worth pausing and just checking whether or not this is a situation we need to fix, solve or act on. Sometimes we don't actually need to do anything and sometimes we definitely DO need to take action. For example,

- Do you need to complete the project this month? (*possibly yes*)
- Do you need to heal your relationship with your child? (*probably yes*)
- Are you the only one who can do x, y, z? (*probably no*)

If the answer to any of these questions is yes, then continue with the remaining questions to define your purpose and get unstuck.

If the answer to the question is no, then you've gotten unstuck by removing your own expectation that you do something.

Question 2: What do I really want in this situation?

Once you have decided you want to take action, then this is the key question. To answer this, you must step back a little and begin to think about what it is that you are trying to achieve. Create some emotional distance from the situation so you can see clearly. Pay particular attention to the REALLY in this question. This makes this question much more powerful than just "What do I want?"

In Steve's example, his initial answer might have been "get the task done". With this purpose, any delay and procrastination from his daughter were threats to his purpose, which amplified his frustration. Yet to step back, he was able to see some of the bigger picture.

> **Steve**: Yes, I wanted to get the injection done, but I really wanted to minimize the pain and frustration for my daughter (and myself). I wanted her to be able to stop worrying. I wanted it to not be a big event. I wanted it to be easy for her.

This was why stepping back to see the importance of her motivation was so impactful. It allowed Steve and his wife to see solutions that worked towards what everyone really wanted.

What do you really want in your situation?

Question 3: What is important about this purpose?

Motivation matters and the only purpose that will drive you to change your situation and get unstuck is the purpose that matters to you. Not the answer that is "correct" or defined by others' opinions. What is important TO YOU about that purpose? That is the answer that creates motivation. It can be a "dark and ugly" reason like, "I want to be better than so and so." Or "It makes me feel special." Don't judge your answer to this question as "right" or "wrong", just be honest.

What is important to you about your purpose?

Question 4: What actions are in my control?

Life is complex, and there are some things you can control, and some things you cannot. Similarly, there are some situations that you can influence, and others where nothing you do will make a difference.

In other words:

- There are things in life that are in your control.
- Things you can influence.
- And things you cannot control nor influence, you must just accept them.

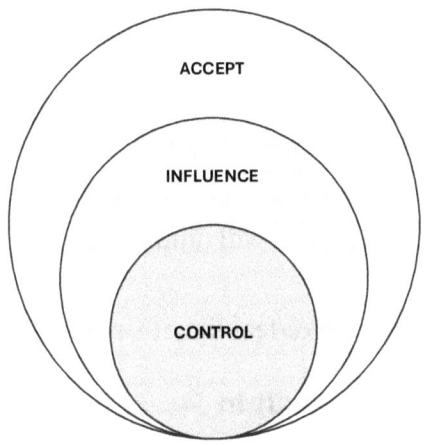

When you mix up what you can control, influence or must accept, you can get incredibly frustrated. You will try to control things you cannot control, or to influence things you cannot influence. You can only change the things you actually control. You control your actions, your thoughts, what you say and what you don't say. You don't control other people, their reactions, or their feelings. And you may or may not even be able to influence those things.

To get unstuck, you must focus, honestly, on what is actually within YOUR control.

The great thing about knowing this is if you are trying to control something and it is not working, you don't get frustrated; just recognize that perhaps you need a different strategy. Perhaps you need to turn to influence! Or just accept that it is here, and let it go all together!

What actions are in my control?

Question 5: What might it look like/feel like if I'm successful?

This isn't a prediction of what WILL happen. It's a description of what might happen, of what is possible. You get to create this possible picture of success. There are no right or wrong answers. What do you hope it looks or feels like if you are successful? This question is important because without thinking of the "finish line", how will you know when you get there? How will you know you have reached the top of the mountain?

This step is also about beginning to get clear on what success looks like which will reinforce the purpose you are seeking.

What might it look like/feel like if I'm successful?

An Example to Lock It In

Let's walk through an example together and then, with your own situation in mind, you'll give it a try.

Here is a simple and common situation - scheduling a doctor's appointment. Imagine you've been feeling sick and had a strange pain in your chest for the past month. You think you need to go see a doctor and get examined, yet you **procrastinate** picking up the phone and calling. Day after day you think about calling and then you don't.

Because you have been procrastinating on calling to book an appointment with the doctor, you decide to try the Using the Power of Purpose tool to get unstuck.

With this task in mind, your answer to these questions might look like this:

1) **What happens if I don't do it?** *I'll continue to worry and be distracted by the pain. I'm not sleeping well because of both the worry and the pain. My family has a history of medical issues, and I'm concerned that if I don't do anything, the problem may get worse or develop into something else. I'll also not have to go to the doctor, which is a good thing, but I'll keep worrying and thinking about it.*

2) **What do I really want in this situation?** *I want to stop worrying about what might be causing the pain. I want to know that it's nothing serious and get relief from the worry and pain.*

3) **What is important about that purpose?** *My worry about what it might be is making me distracted and grumpy. I feel fearful and I don't like that feeling. I also don't like being distracted from my work and when I'm around my family and friends. It is also important to deal with it if there is something wrong. Logically, if there is something wrong, I can fix it. If there is nothing wrong, I can stop worrying.*

4) **What actions are in my control?** *I can't control the outcome of the appointment, but I can control making the appointment and hearing what the doctor has to say. I can control my choice of whether or not to get treatment. I can control my fear. I can focus on feeling better or letting go of worry.*

5) **What might it look like/feel like if I'm successful?** *If I am successful, I will stop procrastinating and call my insurance company right now to find the right kind of doctor and make an appointment. Then, I will feel relief from worry and have a date to look forward to for when I'll hopefully have relief from pain.*

Here are a couple of things to watch for. Notice question #4 about control. That is an important one. Be honest about what you can actually control or influence and intentionally let go of those things that are not in your control, even if you think they should be in your control.

Also, notice that question #5 is not a prediction. It is a possibility, an aspiration. You get to create that outcome and definition of success. There are no right or wrong answers. Define success so that you'll recognize it when you reach it. The more you visualize success, the more you can move towards it. Success is motivating.

When you are creating or clarifying your purpose, you will know that you are on track when it is:

- motivating,
- gives you a wider view, and
- creates multiple pathways forward.

If it does these three things, then it is a good purpose.

Practice

Now it's your turn. Think of the place, situation, or relationship where you feel stuck. What are you avoiding or procrastinating? Use the questions listed here to get to a purpose that is meaningful, motivating, and helpful to you. Pause reading and take notes on your answers to the questions below with your situation in mind.

Using the Power of Purpose:
1) What happens if I don't do it?
2) What do I really want in this situation?
3) What is important about that purpose?
4) What actions are in my control?
5) What might it look like/feel like if I'm successful?

Conclusion

Being stuck means that you cannot see a way to move forward. Using the Power of Purpose to define the "why" of a situation gives you a wider view. By defining your purpose, you not only increase your motivation, but you can also start to see new pathways to get to your destination.

Refocusing on WHY you are doing something allows you to explore the question:

"How do I do the things I don't want to do,

   to get the things I do want to have?"

To define your purpose in a situation, honestly and thoroughly answer these five questions. Your answers will give you the clarity you need.

> **Self-Coaching Questions to Help You Get Unstuck**
>
> Using the Power of Purpose:
> 1) What happens if I don't do it?
> 2) What do I really want in this situation?
> 3) What is important about that purpose?
> 4) What actions are in my control?
> 5) What might it look like/feel like if I'm successful?

For more resources for Using the Power of Purpose and for help creating shared purposes with others, check out www.StuckNoMoreBook.com/Resources using the QR Code below.

CHAPTER 3

I've Tried Everything

"We are what we think. All that we are arises with our thoughts. With our thoughts we make the world." - **Buddha**

"I've tried everything. I can't fix it."

Telling yourself you've tried everything and there is no way forward is a story about what is happening to you. Stories are essential to navigating the world. They help you make sense of the world and help you make decisions about what to do next ... except when that story stops you from seeing solutions and starts to sound like the same negative narrative over and over again. *This is a sign that you are stuck in your story.*

If you are thinking…

- The same thoughts about a particular person or situation over and over again, like an audio file on loop
- A dialogue on repeat and the story you are telling yourself about the situation or the other person isn't helping you move forward

Or if you are feeling…

- frustration
- anger
- embarrassment
- hopelessness
- defensiveness, or
- toxicity each time that story is told in your mind…

Then, the **Changing Your Internal Story** tool will help you…

- identify what isn't working for you in your story
- envision other possibilities, and
- widen your view as a self-coach.

You have an internal story you are telling yourself that isn't working and it's time to change it.

What Are the Self-Coaching Questions to Help You Get Unstuck?

Changing Your Internal Story:

1) What am I focusing on? Who am I blaming?
2) What is the story am I telling myself about what this means?
3) What is it costing me to stay in this story?
4) What is another perspective I could consider?
5) Looking at the situation from this new perspective, how do I feel? What will I do differently as a result?

What Does This Tool Really Mean and How/Why Does it Work?

To understand this tool and how it works, let's first explore the power of stories and the importance of taking a wide-view of things.

Stories Can Be Helpful

People are natural storytellers. From childhood people begin to tell stories – stories about what happened, stories about the meaning of things, stories of dreams, stories from life and stories from our imagination. Stories are so much a part of being human that we often forget that they are there. When we say "story", we are simply referring to a narrative. It's a storyline that connects a series of events or details. It is a story that conveys the meaning in everyday life and helps you make sense of what is happening and why.

Meaning: The depth and type of importance you give to an event, object, person, situation, emotion, or experience. It helps us to answer the questions: Why do I think this happening? What does it mean for me?

Meaning is personal and created by how you feel about what you are seeing.

Stories have been part of life forever, just think about Netflix or Disney. Both are businesses built upon stories. Just ask someone how their day was, and they will begin to tell a story. Stories are everywhere and they bring meaning to the world. In fact, this paragraph is its own form of story. Think, for just a moment, how excited you would be to read this book if it were only a list of key points. No connection and no story would bring no excitement and no engagement from you as the reader.

Stories can entertain, give purpose and meaning and even save you. As it recently saved Steve and his family.

> **Steve**: I was driving on a large, multi-lane highway. There were six lanes in each direction and lots of cars, all traveling at around 70mph. As I was driving, a particular car caught my attention. I don't know what it was that I saw, but my 'radar' was up. There was something about this car that wanted me to pay attention to it. Perhaps it was the type of car, or the license plate, or maybe it was something about the driver, in any case, I just knew that this car was a danger, and I needed to be watchful. The car was just ahead of me, driving in the fast (inside) lane and I just knew that this was one of those drivers who wait until the last second to quickly rush across all lanes and zip into the exit.
>
> Having created this story about the car, I slowed down a little to give it space. I thought, "if they are going to cut in front of me to take the exit at the last moment, then I will be ready for them". It meant that I needed to watch them and be wary.
>
> As a result, I was ready when it happened! One moment, we were all driving nicely in our lanes and the next, ZIP, this car swerved violently and shot across all 5 lanes toward the exit ramp. The driver did not care if there were any cars in the way. The driver just saw the exit and took it. To avoid a crash, some cars had to jam on the brakes, but not me. I was ready. My story had allowed me to prepare for the outcome I expected, ensuring I could respond effectively, and keep my family safe.

As you can see, Steve was telling himself a **story** about this car and what it would do. In this case, his story was useful and helped him make sense of what was happening on the road. Because his story was accurate, Steve was ready when the car zipped across in front of him.

Stories help us describe the connections between all of the different things happening in our complex world. Our stories help us to make sense and to begin to make predictions so that we can prepare for what might happen next. Just like Steve did.

Making sense of your world is essential. It helps you understand what is happening, make decisions and know what to do. Stories serve you.

Except when they don't.

For Steve, anticipating the car about to swerve was not the only story he was telling himself.

> **Steve**: I was also making up some other stories about the driver and why he swerved across 6 lanes. I was also telling myself that:
>
> o   The driver was stupid and selfish.
>
> o   The driver was unsafe and shouldn't be driving.
>
> o   The driver had no respect for anyone but themselves!

These labels and judgments are also stories that you tell yourself about what happened, why it happened and the meaning (that you are creating) behind what happened. Though, because the stories are filled with judgment and blame, they can start to contaminate other stories, leading you to make mistakes and get stuck.

When your stories are accurate, they help you navigate your world. But, when they do not match reality, you get stuck. It happens all the time. You face moments when what you think is happening is not what is actually going on.

I've Tried Everything

Here is a common story that I bet you have gotten stuck in at least once in your life.

> You are in a hurry, rushing to exit a room. You push on the door, expecting it to swing open, but it doesn't budge. Confused, you push harder, feeling a wave of frustration begin to rise in your chest. Your mind races—"What's wrong with this door?!" You grit your teeth and lean your whole body into it. Pushing harder, you are determined to force it open. The pressure builds as your annoyance grows. Then, suddenly, your eyes catch a small sign, right in front of you, right next to the handle. It clearly says, "PULL." A flush of embarrassment washes over you. You pause, take a breath, and gently pull the door open, glancing around, hoping no one noticed your unnecessary struggle.

While amusing (at least when we see others do it), similar situations happen to all of us. Let's slow things down and have another look at this Door example, this time through the lens of Story. As we move through the story, notice how each conclusion leads to another action. Remember, even if you are not aware of the story, it still influences your next steps.

As you rush towards the exit, you looked at the door, unconsciously filtering out information that didn't appear relevant. You saw that the door was closed and that you would need to open it. Based on your vast experience with doors, you connected the information that you had, created some meaning, and decided that the way to do this was to push the door open.

Now you don't know exactly what you saw that led to this conclusion, but it doesn't matter. In what you saw, your experience recognized your reality. You interpreted the situation and clearly this door needed pushing. Importantly, this story allowed you to make sense of what was happening, which meant that you could also make some predictions about what you could do to influence the situation, namely, that if you pushed on the door, it would open.

Based on this story, you did what makes complete sense and pushed the door. But this didn't work. You pushed it and it should have opened, but it didn't - what could this mean? Well, you've already decided that it was a PUSH door, so it pushing it is not working, then it must mean that you didn't push hard enough. Still didn't work! The door must be broken, or something is stuck, so you push harder. Still didn't work. Now you are getting upset, because if you push a door three times, and it still doesn't open, then something must be really wrong, and the owners of the property must be negligent. Somebody has not been doing their job. AND you are getting later with every second. There are places you need to be, and standing here, pushing a broken door is not one of them.

By now, you are really getting angry, because not only does the door not work, but it is also broken AND someone is being lazy and incompetent AND this is making you late. Everything you have seen seems to confirm that your story is correct. It makes perfect sense and because it does, you stick with the story, filter out information that is not relevant, and keep going.

Wow. Let's take a breath. Even just reading this is stressful. The longer this story goes the more stressed you become. You can feel what it is like to be like the person in the story. In this story, the person became stuck in a narrow-view story, and the more intense the emotions become, the narrower the view also becomes.

Narrow-view Story. A story with meaning that contains one perspective and a set of assumptions that generate a high emotional temperature and/or feelings of "stuckness". Narrow-view Stories exclude important information, which leads to the higher emotional temperature and further narrowing of the view.

The challenge with the **narrow-view** is that by repeating the same story over and over, you end up focusing only on information that confirms your story, and thus reinforces your narrow view. The more that you do this, the more your **emotional temperature** rises and the narrower your view becomes. In addition to this, because you are so narrowly focused, you are unintentionally dismissing the broader, **wide-view** that holds the key information to solve your problem – just like being able to see the "Pull" sign on the door, which was there all along.

> **Emotional Temperature.** The intensity of negative emotions within oneself. The more intense, the "higher" the temperature.

Makes sense, right?

Being in the narrow-view is a downward spiral. It is a sticky place because of three specific reasons.

1) **Narrow Focus.** Humans are hard-wired to focus. With so much information around you, you need to **filter out** any information that doesn't seem to matter and **filter in** the information that does. Under stress, or when your **emotional temperature** is high, the filtering increases and you focus on what you perceive to be THE most important thing in the moment – whatever you see as the cause of your emotion! In an attempt to deal with the emotional state, you filter out more and more information.

2) **Automatic Assigning of Meaning.** Life happens so fast that you don't have time to analyze and evaluate everything that happens. Instead, you use your life experiences to look for familiar patterns that can help you quickly make sense of what is happening in life. The easiest way to do this is for you to look for patterns that you recognize, i.e. those you have experienced before. When you see something familiar, you can stop looking, because you 'know' what is happening. When this works, it saves you time and energy. When it doesn't work, you misinterpret the situation, assign incorrect meaning, and become trapped in limited options. In

these situations, your actions are misaligned with reality which creates additional stress as you now have to deal with the situation AND why your actions are not working!

3) **Assuming Your View is the Only Correct View.** Having done all of this work to filter the information, and then searched it for familiar patterns, you then tend to believe that your personal perspective is correct. You forget that your understanding of the situation is created, and that you ignored information to create it (filtering out). This means that there are always alternate ways to look at a situation, alternate views that others hold, and alternate perspectives that you can hold. Your emotional attachment to your current view traps you in your story and leads you to dismiss different ways of seeing.

When you find yourself trapped in a **narrow-view**, it is important to create some emotional distance. To slow down and reduce the emotional temperature allows you to slowly let go of the narrow view and begin to see more of what is happening around (and within) you. Now you can see the **wide-view story**.

Wide-view Story. A story with meaning that includes multiple perspectives of other people, of different angles, and/or different assumptions. It usually contains a variety of potential solutions and is less emotionally charged than a Narrow-view Story. Because they are broader, Wide-view Stories give us access to more information, helping us to get unstuck and move forward.

Let's return to the Door Story and look a bit wider.

> Pushing the door wasn't working and frustrations were rising, until something prompted you to take a wider view. To see beyond your story.
>
> Taking the wider view allowed you to gather more information and to see the sign that says PULL. Now, this sign had been there all along. It didn't just magically appear. It was there at the beginning, but you had filtered this information out. When you looked at the door, you had automatically dismissed that information because it seemed irrelevant, so it didn't even register in your conscious mind. So, you ignored it. Well, you ignored it until you took a wide-view and let that information in.
>
> The new information allowed you to see the situation with a clarity that was not possible from inside your **narrow-view**. This clarity helped you to let go of the escalating emotion and solutions that were previously invisible, suddenly became obvious. PULL!

In this story, you were stuck in the narrow view, pushing and pushing, getting more and more frustrated, until something prompted you to open up your awareness. The story doesn't tell us what happened to help you open up your view. It just seemed to happen. One moment the door was stuck, and the next there was a sign saying 'PULL'.

> **The Narrow-view Story** is, "The door is stuck, I need to push harder. It's still not opening, I will push even harder. It is still not working!!! Now I am late and I am getting mad."
>
> **A Wide-view Story** could be, "the door is stuck. I know am late and rushing to get out, let me take a breath and see why it might be sticking. There

might be some other information to help me get out."

Earlier we listed the three reasons it's easy to get stuck in a narrow-view story. Let's briefly explore each one in more detail. Understanding each of these reasons will help you overcome them and connect you back to a wide-view story. This way you can get unstuck and create better solutions in your life.

Humans Have a Narrow Focus

Just like in a photograph, focus helps bring clarity to what you are looking at. More than this, you select your focus based on what you are doing. In the modern world, this is an essential skill, because there is so much information around us.

For just a moment, think about all of the different sources of information available to you:

- Physical (external) senses like eyes, ears, taste, smell, touch
- Internal world, emotions, thoughts, worries, desires, physical needs
- People around you, how they look, what they are doing, saying, thinking
- Physical environment, birds, waves, trees, traffic, neighbors, alarms
- Internet, social media, email, news feeds, music, books, games

Imagine how exhausting it would be, and how much you would (or would not) get done if you had to pay attention to everything, all at once, all of the time!

Thankfully, part of your survival instinct as a human is to be able to hyper-focus your attention. This means that you can narrow down your focus, paying attention to a small group of things, while also excluding almost everything else. Most of the time, this works well and helps you to focus on relevant information. However, sometimes you end up filtering out important information that leads you to becoming stuck in a narrow story. This becomes more likely when you are stressed, or your emotional temperature is high.

The problem is not THAT you filter out information. The problems emerge when you end up filtering out IMPORTANT information.

Let's explore this using the example of taking a photo.

> When you decide to take a photo, there are some steps that you take before you actually snap the picture. First, you decide what you want to take the photo of. Is it the person in front of you, is it the building behind them, or is it the fireworks in the sky? You need to choose what is important to have IN the picture. Then, you need to choose what you DO NOT WANT in the picture. You choose what information you want to filter out. To do this, you zoom in, you change how you frame your subject, and you move so that you get the right light, the right angles, and the right composition. And finally, if there is a person in the picture, you ask them to pose/smile so that they look their best in the image.

While this is a very deliberate example, you automatically follow these steps in most things that you focus on.

You have a view of life, or of a person or a situation. You choose what you want to focus on (include) and what to filter out (exclude). You do this based on what you are doing and what you think is important in the moment. The picture that you end up with, based on what you filtered, leads you to build a story to make sense of what is happening. This story then informs you about which other information to include or ignore.

Obviously, if your 'picture' of reality is based on limited information, then your view of reality is limited and so is the story you create about that view.

In the case of a narrow-view, the story that is created causes problems because it tells you to look in one direction, ignoring all others. If you want to expand from a narrow-view to a wide-view, then you need to change your story to help you include more of the information that you had previously been ignoring. You must change your focus.

Narrow-view

With a narrow-view, the situation appears to be a girl smelling a flower.

A Wide-view

With a wide-view, you can see that the situation is a boy giving a bouquet of flowers to a girl. Wider-view, different story.

How you are feeling and thinking affects what gets filtered in and what gets filtered out. When your **emotional thermometer** is high, your focus narrows and more information is excluded.

This means that as your emotional temperature rises, your view becomes more and more narrow. And you get stuck.

To get unstuck, you need to expand how you see - to shift your story to a Wide-view Story. One thing that really helps with this, is to look at the meaning that you are using to filter new information.

You Automatically Create Meaning

The second reason that you get stuck in the **Narrow-view** Story is that you automate how you make meaning of what you are seeing in life.

With so much information coming towards you, you would soon be overwhelmed if you had to pay attention to all of the blades of grass or every movement of every muscle in your body. You'd be overwhelmed if you had to listen to all of the bird noises, the cars driving past, the footstep sounds of those passing by, and the wind in the trees. If you had to pay attention and integrate all of that, you would never get anywhere.

For humans to survive, we need to filter stuff out, which means you need a way of prioritizing what's important and what's relevant. You need a way to quickly determine what information will impact you, and what will not.

Thankfully, you have a quick and simple way of doing this - you look at what you see around you and use it to create a story that explains what is going on. This story will tell you about the situation, the characters, their motivations, and will point to what is going to happen next. This allows you to interact with your world, and to make a difference. It can be very helpful to quickly create these stories except when they leave out important information and leave us stuck.

In the earlier Door Story, you looked at the door, and recognized that if you were to push, the door would open. While the story was wrong, having a story helped you take the next step. You pushed. And the door didn't open. You didn't get the result you wanted and had an opportunity to re-evaluate your story.

Your stories will never be completely the same as what is happening in your life because stories are built on limited information. This works for you most of the time because your stories are close enough. Normally, close enough is good enough and as you progress in a situation, you can learn more and adjust your story as you go.

As we saw earlier with Steve's example, he had the story of what was happening which allowed him to predict the sudden movement of the car. He also had another, emotional layer where he was judging the driver as stupid and inconsiderate.

This second layer of meaning creation is what raises your emotional temperature. It's the **meaning** that causes the pain, disappointment, anger, fear, joy, connection, love, etc. It's not what happens to you that matters, it's what you do with it that counts. It's true. And one of the first things that you do with any situation is assign a meaning to it.

In other words, it's not the red traffic light that causes your frustration. It's the meaning you assign to having to wait the extra 2 minutes at that light that causes frustration. The meaning that says, "now I'll be late. And I'll feel embarrassed and uncomfortable. I hate being late and this red light is making me late. I hate this red light."

Think about the following example:

Imagine sending an important text message to a close friend and they don't respond. Hours go by and still nothing.

What could this mean?

> **Negative Story**: They should have responded by now. If they haven't responded, they must be upset with you. Now you examine the details of every recent interaction, finding the reasons why they might be upset. A tone, a word, perhaps that time you interrupted.
>
> But, no, you haven't done anything wrong, they have no reason to be upset about you, in fact they should be apologizing.
>
> You get frustrated, angry, defensive and feel abandoned.
>
> As a result, you send a series of follow-up messages that are abrupt and defensive, further straining the situation. The silence continues making you feel anxious and isolated.

Notice how the negative story amplifies the feeling. Just like we saw in the Door Story.

> **Positive Story**: Perhaps your friend is just busy and while the message was important, you continue with your day.
>
> You remain calm and patient, trusting that you'll get a reply when your friend is free.
>
> When the friend finally replies, you can respond warmly and without tension, preserving the positive connection in your relationship.

By comparison, this positive story is kind of boring. It is as if nothing happened. There is no emotional spiral.

As you can see by this simple example, nothing in the situation has changed, yet when we change the story, everything is different. Meaning is created.

This is good news. When you find yourself in a 'negative story', you can change it. If the meaning you are creating doesn't make things better, widen your view and find a new way to see things.

> *"When you change the way you look at things, the things you look at change"*
> Dr Wayne Dyer

While this is good news, it is also true that you can become very attached to your view of the world and the meanings that you have created. Even if they are misaligned to reality or lead you into an emotional spiral.

You Believe Your View is Correct

At this point in your life, you probably believe you are a sane, mature, capable adult who sees the world correctly. You see things as they are. Sometimes you let others add to, or expand your view, but your way of seeing things is correct. As you have read, the story that you are telling yourself informs how you filter information, which reinforces your story. This means that within a particular perspective, you will continually seek to validate and confirm that your understanding of the world is correct.

This is great. It helps you have confidence and clarity in how you see the world, allowing you to quickly respond to changes and to take actions that make sense. This also means that you will strongly defend your perspective to others, because you believe yourself more than you believe anyone else. Sometimes this is fun, like knowing that your sporting team IS better than the opposition - obviously, fans of the opposition believe the opposite, but **they** are clearly wrong!

Being wrong isn't a problem. It is easy to correct your perspective with new information when you are not emotionally tied to your original idea ... even if you have held that perspective for a long time.

For example, Steve recently visited the pyramids in Giza, Egypt.

> **Steve**: Before I arrived in Egypt, I had a very clear idea of what I was going to see. For years, even back in primary school, I had seen pictures of these fabulous monuments to the Pharaohs. Giant pyramids in the middle of the desert, surrounded by sand and camels. A little like the picture below.

https://www.planetware.com/tourist-attractions-/pyramids-of-giza-egy-giza-giza.htm

> When I arrived, however, I was surprised to find that they weren't in the middle of the desert. I was able to see the pyramids as I was driving through the city. This is what I saw.

https://sacredsites.com/africa/egypt/the_great_pyramid_of_giza.html

I was surprised to see shops and hotels right across the road from these ancient monuments. I had no idea that the Great Pyramids were on the edge of the city. If you had tried to tell me it was true, I would not have believed you and argued strongly that you were wrong. Everyone knows the pyramids are out in the middle of the desert.

But a wider-view reveals the truer picture.

https://en.wikipedia.org/wiki/Pyramid

Because I was not emotionally tied to my view, I was able to easily change my perspective to include the new information. In fact, I was able to see humor in changing my perspective.

As you can see, depending on your view, the pyramids are not as huge as you imagined them to be.

I could touch the top! (or could I?)

Problems emerge, however, when your view is misaligned with what is happening around you, and you become so attached to your current view that you resist any other ways of seeing.

When emotional temperature is high your view is much more difficult to let go of because logical information holds no weight in an emotional argument. Emotionally driven views are more resistant to change even in the face of new data, at least until you change your emotional temperature.

> Imagine for a minute that you have a boss, and you have heard him shout at you and your colleagues for not delivering on time, or for making mistakes. You have seen this boss make uncaring decisions

to increase profit even though it hurts the people around you. Unsurprisingly, you might develop a view that your boss doesn't care about people, he only cares about business outcomes.

This might make you feel emotionally charged, because now you believe you are one of those people he doesn't care about. From that point on, every time you see your boss, you will look for evidence to support this story that he is uncaring and only cares about the numbers.

Imagine that one day, your boss comes to talk with you and begins to give you compliments, telling you what a great job you have been doing in the last few weeks.

Would this change your story about him? Would you say to yourself, "Oh no! I was wrong, he is wonderful and caring." OR, would you maintain the story and try to work out what he is trying to get from you or make you do?

If you are like most people, you will fall into the second category, and will be inclined to interpret his actions as "just trying to get you to work harder or longer to make sure that you get the numbers." And so, your story gets reinforced. Even if he is nice this time, you will probably discount his kindness before you change your story.

Why do you do this?

First, you are not motivated to change your view because you believe it is correct and you have strong emotions involved in the situation.

Second, through this view, you will seek information and evidence that supports the view. You'll look for information that proves that your view is correct. More than this, you will tend to interpret all the information around you in ways that also reinforce your view. This is called the Confirmation Bias, and it's natural and it's human. It just doesn't always serve you very well.

When your boss asks about business data, you naturally interpret his question as proof that he only cares about the numbers.

When you see him talking kindly to another employee, you are inclined to interpret his actions as "he only cares about her to get her to work harder to create the numbers" and your view gets stronger.

Like a stone being pulled to the earth by gravity, a narrow-view story sits heavy in your mind and heart. It takes a lot of energy to lift and move your story to a higher or wider place.

However, the secret to shifting is simple. Not necessarily easy, mind you, but definitely simple.

You Can Change Your Story

Let's see this in action. Have a look at the following image.

What do you see?

Gestalt Principles of Perception

Do you see a lady's face?

Do you see the shadow of a Saxophone player?

Now that we have asked the questions, can you see both images?

The lady's face is white, with black eyes, nose, and mouth with her black hair, or perhaps, shadow on the left. And the saxophone player in black, is on the left of the image.

This is an example of an ambiguous picture. It is ambiguous because the image can be interpreted as two different patterns, to mean two different things. Your mind is fantastic at looking at patterns and coming up with a meaning. It does this by looking at the information in context of what is around it. Context helps to make the meaning, and where context is unclear, ambiguous, or not present, then you automatically pick the context based on how you are feeling.

Have a look at the drawing of a box. Which face of the box is closest to you?

Can you see the two different ways that this can be interpreted?

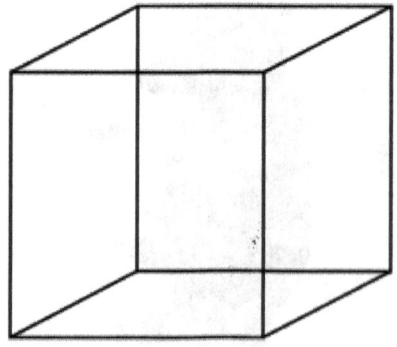

The first way is as if this box is flat on a table, and we are looking at it from the side.

The second way appears that we are looking down on the box from the top.

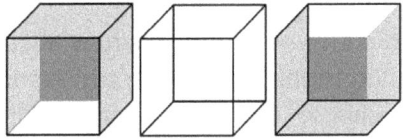

Choose which way you want to look at the image and see if you can switch between them.

Here is another example known as Schröder's Stairs. As you look at this image, answer the question, which face (A or B) is closer to you?

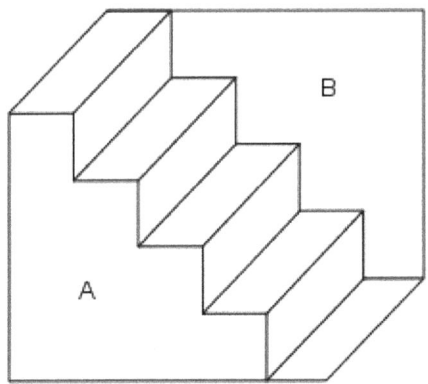

Many people will initially say that side A is in front. As they do this, they will also see that the image looks like a set of stairs that someone could walk down from left to right. In this view, B is the back wall of the stairs.

Now try to see side B as being in front of side A. In this view, side B will almost be popping out of the page, and we are now looking up at the underside of the stairs. Or perhaps it feels more like a cliff with B on top, and the cube cut cliff wall dropping down to the floor at A.

While this can be tricky for some, play with it and notice that just by thinking differently, you can change how you see the image - you change the meaning.

The same is true for you in life. There is always more than one way of interpreting what is happening and while you automatically choose one way, you can change it if it doesn't serve you.

You can choose to change your story by changing the meaning you assign to "facts" in your story. With these images, you just did that very thing!

Changing Your Internal Story to get Unstuck

Understanding that stories can serve you or get in your way is the first step to seeing better solutions to the challenges and frustrations in your life.

To change your Internal Story, you need to do two things.

1) Reduce your emotional temperature.
2) Change the story you are telling yourself.

The good news is that reducing your emotional temperature and Changing Your Internal Story work hand in hand. Reduce your emotional temperature by shifting:

- where you focus
- the meaning you are assigning, and
- be open to other perspectives.

As you do this, your story automatically begins to change. You'll start to see a wide-view story that changes how you feel and think about that person or situation as you:

- overcome the human tendency to narrowly focus
- widen your view
- see what the others see
- feel what others feel, and

- understand others' intentions.

So, How Do I Use Changing Your Internal Story?

Here are the questions to ask and answer for yourself when you are stuck in your story and are unable to see how to move forward. These are the initial questions to ask, but keep digging and asking yourself follow-up questions until you suddenly see something you hadn't seen before - and that something leads you to a new solution that you can try.

1) What am I focusing on? Who am I blaming?
2) What is the story am I telling myself about what this means?
3) What is it costing me to stay in this story?
4) What is another perspective I could consider?
5) Looking at the situation from this perspective, how do I feel? What will I do differently as a result?

Next Level: Remembering what you've read in the Power of Purpose chapter, you can utilize the power of purpose here to widen your story by also asking yourself these questions:

6) What is the ending to this story that I want to have happen?
7) What is one step I can take toward that new ending?

An Example to Lock It In

Here is an example from Lisa on how to use the questions to see your internal story and change it. Have you been or are you currently in a similar situation? How could these questions help you?

> **Lisa**: I can't even remember now what it was that set me off but, I was at home and my husband spoke to me in a way that immediately triggered me. Oh

wow. I went from feeling fine and neutral to feelings of anger and a boiling point in emotional temperature in about 3 seconds! I knew I needed to work it out before I said anything that I might regret. So, I practically ran out the door and advised my husband that I was, "just going for a walk".

As I dashed from the house, my thoughts were flying faster than my feet.

"I can't believe he would speak to me that way! Who does he think he is!? Who does he think I am!? I am not the kind of woman who has a husband who would speak to her that way! No way!! If that's really what he thinks of me, then I don't see how we can even continue in this relationship. Unbelievable!"

Yes I know. It sounds a little extreme. In a matter of minutes, I went from happily married to the brink of divorce in my own head. But perhaps you can relate. In that moment, what he said and how I felt about it became a very real, very intense story with only one way out.

As I walked, and fumed, I noticed how quickly I had gone from, "I love my life and my husband," to "I can't be married to someone who believes that about me!"

Luckily, before I opened my mouth and told my husband our marriage was over, I created some physical distance by going for a walk. This helped me to cool down and gave me a chance to coach myself and check my story. It sounded something like this:

"Okay Lisa, hold on. **What are you focusing on and who are you blaming?**"

"Obviously it's not just his words, it's what he believes about me that would cause him to say those words! That is what I'm rightly focusing on. The feeling behind his words. If that is how he feels, then that is how he feels. But I can't believe I'm in a relationship with someone like that. I'm not the kind of woman who can be with a man who speaks to me that way and thinks that of me. If I stay, I'll blame myself for allowing it to continue."

"What is the story you are telling yourself about what this means?"

"Uh...it means I cannot stay with him and simultaneously be the kind of woman I believe I am. A woman who is respected and who respects herself."

"What is it costing you to stay in this story?"

"Well, if I stay in this story, it will cost me my marriage."

"Okay. So, before you blow up the best relationship you've ever had, take a moment. **What is another perspective you could consider?** Like your husband's perspective perhaps?"

"I heard what I heard but...maybe, just maybe, he didn't mean what I think he meant by those words. I can't imagine what else he might have meant, it seemed pretty clear. But, I'm open to the possibility that he meant something different."

"Looking at the situation from this perspective, how do you feel? What will you do differently as a result?"

"I feel relieved that there is a possible way out that doesn't require the death of my relationship. I feel open to a different interpretation of his words and willing to ask him, without judgment or anger, what he meant. I'm going to ask."

It took me 4 laps around the pond near my house to work through my story. The questions enabled me to look inside myself and figure out why I was really mad, calm down, get open to a different possibility and re-enter the house with love, not anger, in my heart.

I anchored into what I knew from past experiences with my husband, not what I interpreted in the story I was telling myself from this current experience. Once I felt calm, open, and more curious than angry, I went back into the house.

My husband greeted me with a smile, and I simply asked, "I heard you say *this*, did you mean *that*?" He was surprised. "No way!", he said. "I meant *this* and *this*."

I was able to see a wide-view and respond, "Oh yes, I can see that now. I heard *this*. Thanks for clarifying."

The crisis was averted. Escalation was avoided. And, resolution and insight were achieved. Phew!

Conclusion

Stories help you make sense of the world. Sometimes the story you are telling yourself isn't true. And sometimes it isn't the only story.

Examining the stories you tell yourself when you are stuck or frustrated can help you get unstuck.

Now it's your turn. Think of a challenging situation or relationship where you feel stuck, the emotional temperature is high and/or you believe there is no way for the situation to change. With that situation or relationship in mind, ask yourself the following questions and answer them honestly! If you really want to see success, write down your answers.

> **Self-Coaching Steps to Help You Get Unstuck**
>
> Using Changing Your Internal Story:
>
> 1) What am I focusing on? Who am I blaming?
> 2) What is the story am I telling myself about what this means?
> 3) What is it costing me to stay in this story?
> 4) What is another perspective I could consider?
> 5) Looking at the situation from this perspective, how do I feel? What will I do differently as a result?

Next Level: Remembering what you've read in the Power of Purpose chapter, you can utilize the power of purpose here to widen your story by also asking yourself these questions:

6) What is the ending to this story that I want to have happen?
7) What is one step I can take toward that new ending?

For more resources for Changing Your Internal Story, check out www.StuckNoMoreBook.com/Resources using the QR Code below.

CHAPTER 4

The Pressure is Too Much

"Pressure can burst a pipe or create a diamond. What it does in your life is up to you." - Lisa C Gregory and Dr. Steve Jeffs

"The pressure is too much!"

We all feel pressure in our lives. Pressure can inspire us to get things done, to be productive and to create amazing outcomes. Pressure can also be too much, leaving us feeling fearful, overwhelmed, exhausted and questioning everything.

When the pressure is too much, sometimes we collapse and crumble under it. On the other hand, for many of us, feeling this pressure is an indicator that we need to go harder, to push through 'the pain'. Unfortunately, what can happen is that the more overwhelmed we are, the more the 'push through' mindset becomes our everyday way of being, where the drive to achieve dominates our lives.

This chapter will help you balance your driving pressure to achieve, with energy-creating activities and relationships. It will help you re-energize yourself, your work, your relationships, and your life while still creating the achievement and success that is important to you.

It is time to use the **Refocusing the Pressure to Achieve** tool when the feeling of pressure is getting to be too much or is always present.

This tool is for you if you are feeling…

- overwhelmed
- burned out
- tired
- worried
- stressed
- frustrated

And this tool is for you if you are thinking…

- "Why do I have to do everything?"
- "Why can't anyone else get it right?"
- "When will I finally see the success I want?"
- "I don't think I even know how to relax anymore."

This chapter will help you exit this vicious cycle and create the balance you need. You will be able to increase your energy and your joy in life and work. And, it will help you see how to create more of the success in life that matters to you.

What Are the Self-Coaching Questions to Help You Get Unstuck?

Refocusing The Pressure to Achieve:

1) What is my personal performance measure in this situation/relationship? What does it mean to "perform"?

2) What brings me energy as I create performance?
3) What decreases my energy?
4) What can I do to increase my energy even more?
5) How will I know when I have both energy and performance?
    a) What will I do? How will I feel? What results will I get (in both energy and performance?)
6) What is my insight and next step?

What Does This Tool Really Mean and How/Why Does it Work?

To understand this tool and how it works, let's first explore what achievement means and how a common definition of achievement often gets us stuck.

Achievement is important. As parents we drive our kids to learn, act and achieve. At work we have tasks to deliver and outcomes to achieve.

The pressure to achieve drives your success, learning and growth. Feeling pressure has helped you to create some amazing successes in your life. As an achiever, this pressure has also been too much at times and has created high stress, issues with your health, fatigue and many negative emotions.

Pressure is a double-edged sword. When there is no pressure, energy is too low. This often means that performance is also low as we have little motivation and don't really care about what we are doing. So, no pressure is not the answer. From a place of boredom, increasing the pressure to achieve will increase performance on difficult or complex activities. We know this, and this is exactly why we drive ourselves forward. Because we believe that increasing pressure increases performance, we do this to ourselves, our teams and our kids – we increase the pressure, hoping to drive performance.

Unfortunately, we forget that increasing pressure to increase performance only works when the pressure to achieve is too low. It works, but only up to a point. After this point, any increase in pressure becomes stress and anxiety and decreases the quality and quantity of our performance. We need to implement different strategies based upon where we are.

In graphic form, it looks like this:

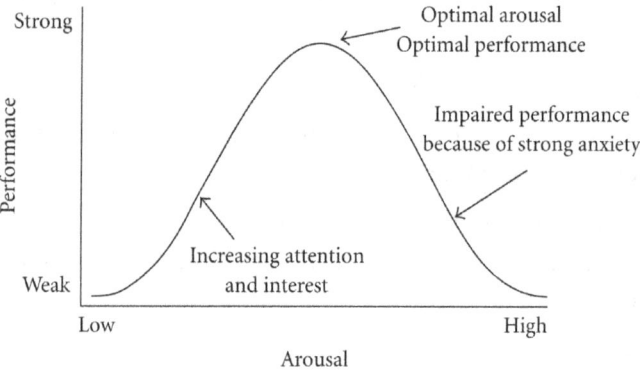

Yerkes-Dodson Law - Wikipedia

If our "arousal" is low and we are bored, more pressure can increase performance. When the task is challenging, and we are stressed and anxious, then we need a different solution. In that situation, we need a solution that reduces arousal and allows us to reconnect to inner energy and resources.

Something To Think About

The Yerkes-Dodson Law, graphed above, shows how your level of arousal informs your level of performance. The optimal level of arousal for best performance varies depending on the nature of the task and your individual characteristics. More is not always better!

So, if you want more performance (of tasks and relationships), then pay attention to whether you have too little, too much, or just the right level of arousal.

The pressure to achieve drives us forward, until we see that we aren't achieving as much as we want, then the pressure increases, and we work harder to achieve. Ironically that extra pressure then slows us down, as we feel it sucking the energy and life out of us. We don't make enough progress and get stuck looking at all of the things that we still haven't achieved.

To use a metaphor, think of the pressure to achieve as a car engine. When there is pressure to achieve, we want to go fast so we push hard on the gas (accelerator). Pushing harder on the gas makes the car go faster, so it makes sense that we push hard. Yet sometimes, pushing harder means that the wheels start to spin. When the wheels spin the engine is working hard, yet the car is barely moving. If the car is not moving, what we tend to do (in life) is push harder on the gas to get it going faster. When the wheels are spinning, this only amplifies the problem, and the car still goes nowhere, yet the wheels spin faster and the engine works harder.

In life, the solution is not necessarily to work harder, but to focus our energy so that it can make a difference. With the car, taking your foot off the gas creates an opportunity for the wheels to gain traction, and thus propel you forward.

The big question of this chapter is what can you do when you find yourself stretched beyond the point of optimal performance and your wheels are spinning?

A Common Definition of Success

When you are experiencing too much pressure, have a look at how you define success. If you are stuck, you probably have a definition that says you must have achieved your goals to be successful.

Achievement = Success

Notice that in this definition the only achievement that counts is the one that is done. You need to finish; you need to complete in order to achieve. But then there is always another incomplete achievement sitting behind that one, and more behind that.

With this definition, success is an unnamed "standard" that is ambiguous and vague. It is like a finish line at the end of the rainbow which continually moves away from us and is impossible to reach.

The result?

STRESS!

And a nagging and persistent feeling that you have not achieved enough.

When **Achievement = Success**, you sacrifice energy, time, relationships, and joy, to chase the unattainable 'achievement'. You work harder, do a bit more and deliver in the short term, with long term energy and relationship depletion. The drive to reach this achievement of success pressures you to work harder because you can continually see all of the things that have not yet been achieved. You can clearly see all that has not been done. And, as this continues over time, you actually achieve less, have less energy, all while experiencing more burnout and more frustration.

Wow. Even reading that last paragraph is exhausting. Yet there are many people living their lives like this, maybe even you. You achieve the pressing things on your list, but you still feel that something is missing. At the end of the day, you feel drained and empty instead of accomplished and excited about tomorrow.

"Achievement = Success" is not enough.

When you define success as achievement, and achievement as success, you miss everything that is important.

This way of defining success doesn't include how you feel. It ignores any sense of whether you are enjoying what you are doing, or if you even **feel** successful. It's also really easy to fall into the trap of thinking that once you have achieved, then you will feel good.

It doesn't work that way. Feeling is an experience not a destination, and life wants us to feel along the way, not just after all is said and done.

Even if you flip the formula around, it is not enough.

Success = Achievement is also incomplete.

Achievement alone is not enough. You need a more powerful and accurate definition of success - one that includes energy and joy, as well as tasks and relationships - the good stuff of life! With a more powerful definition of success, you can actually feel successful!

How to Successfully Define Success

Success is a feeling, not a destination.

Before we give you our definition, take a moment to find your own true definition of how it feels when you are successful.

Think back to a moment when you felt successful. A moment when you were enjoying the task or relationship and felt energized and engaged in what you were doing. A moment when you were happy and excited with the progress you were making and the outcomes you were achieving.

1) What were you doing?
2) What results did you create?
3) What did the process of creating those results feel like?
4) What were your relationships with those involved like?
5) How did you feel?
6) What was your energy like while you were achieving?

Here is an example of how Steve has answered the questions above to define his success in a recent situation.

1. What were you doing?

The first image I have was when I was on a ski slope learning how to snowboard. I can actually picture myself halfway up the hill, standing still and about to move forward.

2. What results did you create?

I was learning. I was focused on what I was doing, and I was getting better. Sure, I would fall, but each time I did, I was able to recognize what I was doing wrong or wasn't doing right and this helped me to get better as I progressed down the hill.

3. What did the process of creating those results feel like?

It felt great to see my progress and to recognize how I was different at the bottom of the hill than I was at the top. It was also exhilarating as I was able to spend more and more time snowboarding, and less time falling and standing up again.

4. **What were your relationships with those involved like?**

    In this example it was just me on the hill (working by myself but surrounded by others also skiing/snowboarding). Yet, I can see a successful relationship between myself, my physical body, and the hill. I wasn't judgmental of my failures, I was present and open to learning and I accepted that while my brain (thought it) knew what to do, I was there to coordinate all of my muscles to actually do it.

5. **How did you feel?**

    Present, motivated, and driven.

6. **What was your energy like while you were achieving?**

    I had moments of flow, freedom, and excitement - not in a jump up and down sense, but in a "yes, I did it" sense.

Successful people notice that they are at their best when they have a positive impact on what they are doing (performance) AND are energized by their work. This is true, even when what you were doing was really difficult.

Think about it ... there are things in your life where you get good results, but that drain your energy. Even though you are good (or seem to be good) at these things, you procrastinate and dread doing them. That doesn't sound like the definition of success!

The forgotten secret ingredient to success is Energy. It is your energy that makes all the difference. A more powerful definition of success is:

Success = High Energy* + High Performance**

*Energy = physical, mental, and emotional reserves

**Performance = task and/or relational outcomes

Think about this for just a moment. What would life be like if you had high energy, were passionate, engaged, or excited, AND you were performing well? Imagine if you felt that way every day! That is the sort of success you can have more of!

What impact would that have on your achievement? What would it do to your productivity? Your results? Your life?

Compare this with those moments when you are stuck.

How does it feel to be stuck? Energizing? Joyful? A big part of why you are stuck is because you have lost connection to what energizes you.

Refocusing the Pressure to Achieve to include high energy AND high performance transforms success and increases your ability to sustainably achieve. More than that, adding energy to mid-level performance increases performance!

However, simply knowing this definition is not enough. To apply it successfully, you will need to know more about what High Energy and High Performance mean for you in your world, with your tasks, your relationships, your goals and your abilities.

Let's look at high energy first.

> **Something To Think About**
>
> We have already seen (Ch 2) that progress by itself is not enough. Meaning and purpose are essential, yet are often not enough, especially with longer term goals, or those that feel mundane. Yes, you can also redefine the stories you tell yourself (Ch 3), and this works well. So, let's build upon this and pay attention to how you can energize yourself in ways that support your meaningful performance.

Exploring Energy

To understand high energy for yourself, start paying attention to the activities or relationships that bring you energy. What energizes you, even a little?

For many of us, this can be an incredibly difficult question. Not because there is nothing that energizes us, but rather because we have had years of practice ignoring our feelings. When Success is defined as Achievement, we learn to ignore how we feel because it is not important.

More than this, we have learned to ignore our feelings as a survival mechanism because constantly striving for achievement drains our energy. By ignoring these feelings, we risk burning out even faster.

So, give yourself permission to pay attention to what is energizing; to notice those moments where you might find yourself drawn in. Where you lose a sense of time, or where you prioritize these activities over others.

It is important to recognize that we are talking about a sense of energy, fulfillment, or engagement. We are not (necessarily) looking for ecstasy, excitement, or 'fun'. Each of us has a different definition of feeling energized, and now is your opportunity to learn more about what energizes you.

> **Something To Think About**
>
> People often think of working harder as a driver of performance. But working harder often leads to lower energy and lower performance or slower performance. "Work smarter, not harder," is a phrase often said, but the common component there is "work". In your most successful times, you were aware of work, but the overriding experience is one of joy, flow, energy and excitement.

Here are some examples:

- Do you love doing the detailed work necessary for spreadsheets and data analysis?
- Do you love collaborating and sharing ideas?
- Do you feel most energized by those parts of your work that require problem solving?
- Do you feel motivated by working with others toward a common goal?
- Do you feel energized by connecting with others?

Pause and write down your own answers.

Write as many as you can. Be as specific as you can.

Sometimes we love only part of an activity, so remember to look for parts of activities too. Write down the activity, and the parts that energize you.

The Pressure to Achieve: Energy and Performance

List tasks that energize you or that have moments where you feel energy.	List relationships that energize you or that have moments where you feel energy.
1) 2) 3) 4) 5) 6)	1) 2) 3) 4) 5) 6)
List tasks where your performance is high or that have moments where you feel energy	List relationships where your performance is high or that have moments where you feel energy.
1) 2) 3) 4) 5) 6)	1) 2) 3) 4) 5) 6)
Notes:	

There is a downloadable worksheet you can use for this section at www.StuckNoMoreBook.com/Resources.

Have a look at your list. What patterns do you see?

What else are you aware of?

Before we move our attention to performance, we want to expand your definition of activities. When looking for energizing activities, we have found that most people look at tasks that give them some energy. This is great, but not everything. We also want you to look at Relationships. What relationships do you find energizing?

Who are those people you love working with or spending time with?

Make a list of these as well, using your worksheet.

Now, let's explore Performance.

Exploring Performance

Like you just did with activities (tasks and relationships) that energize you, now list the activities where you perform well. You are welcome to define performance however you want at this point. You might think you perform well, or perhaps you have received feedback from others about your high performance.

Either way, write them down.

Now have a look across your Energy and Performance lists on your worksheet.

Which activities do you find on both lists, the ones that have both high energy and high performance? Write these down.

Just to expand your list for now, also write down those areas where you perform well and have some level of energy - it doesn't have to be high, but it doesn't suck.

For those that have both High Energy AND High Performance, these are your key success activities.

Commit to doing more of what brings both high energy AND high performance into your work and life. At least once a day, create success for yourself with this new definition.

You'll find that as you add energy into your definition, you will decrease feeling burned out and overwhelmed. The pressure to achieve against some nameless, unattainable standard will also decrease. You now have a new standard against which to measure your tasks and relationships.

"How am I creating both energy and performance?"

Something To Think About

Remember how you chose an area of your life earlier in the chapter? The one where you'd like to have more success? What was the definition of success you wrote down? Go to the worksheet in the downloadable Resource file and ask yourself the Energy and Performance Self-Coaching Questions about that area.

www.StuckNoMoreBook.com/Resources

Success = High Energy + High Performance

To use this definition to create more success that is meaningful in your life, you'll need to be honest and thoughtful with yourself. Use the self-coaching questions to critically identify those things that actually bring you energy ... not what is "socially acceptable" or superficial. You aren't answering the questions so others will be pleased. Answer them honestly so you can identify the activities, ways of thinking, connecting with others, beliefs and behaviors that bring energy to you instead of sucking it away.

When you know the ingredients to YOUR energy formula, you will be able to consistently and intentionally create more energy in your life as you pursue success!

Before we turn you loose to ask the energy questions of yourself for every arena of your life, there are two more things to think about.

1) How to define success in tasks, and
2) How to define success in relationships.

Defining Success in Tasks and Relationships

1. Success in Tasks

Think of a task or work you do that you love doing, are good at and that brings you energy. It's a task that you would love to do much more often if you could.

What is it?

What is your performance like on this task compared to the average person on the street?

Don't compare yourself to your boss, your colleagues, your peers, or your spouse. What is your performance like compared to the average person at the mall or grocery store?) There IS something that you can do better than the average person does.

What is it?

Own that you DO perform well in certain areas.

Now think, how do you feel when you are doing that work?

Exactly. You are pretty awesome at it, aren't you. It comes easily to you, and you really like it.

What is interesting is that you think you are "normal" and "average" but, there are also things you can do that you are especially good at, and other people can't do as well. "Your" things bring you energy when you do them. You can get lost in the work and time just passes by. It's an activity or task that is in your high energy AND high-performance zone. It's fun, creative, interesting, engaging and when you do it, you just feel like you are "in flow".

That's what those "crazy" people are doing when they say, "If you love what you do, you'll never work a day in your life." They aren't really crazy. The majority of their work is just in their high-energy, high-performance zone. Unlike the rest of us who have slipped out of the "high energy and high-performance zone" and back into "the slog" (depleted energy and acceptable performance).

> **Lisa**: I love working out schedules and logistics. I'm really good at it. I see how things and people can move around in an efficient way to get everything done. It's fun for me, especially when I solve problems that other people are stumped by. My husband, on the other hand, feels drained and overwhelmed by figuring out the details. He likes to think about and plan the big picture and enroll other people in his vision.

There are things you do well and naturally. Own them. Own your own brilliance. By doing so, you can also let go of the things that don't bring you energy, that you aren't great at. Let go of the guilt and the worry. Focus on what you CAN and DO excel at.

About now, there is a little voice in your head saying, "But if you let go of the things you aren't good at, you'll get lazy and won't push yourself and then you'll fail!"

You are so programmed for success that you will never let the wheels fall off the bus, you'll never allow everything to fall apart. That isn't your problem. Your problem is filling your life and time with TOO many things that you aren't naturally good at and not filling it with enough of your energy-creating brilliance! So, tell that little voice to take a hike. That voice has had decades to run your life and look at the results. Some results are really good, even great. Some have come at a steep price. Tell the voice it's time to try something new and different. You can do it.

Taking an inventory of the tasks in your life and noticing what brings you more energy and what drains your energy will be enlightening. We'll use the coaching questions in a few minutes to do that. For now, commit to becoming more aware of the energy in your life and commit to increasing the amount of time you spend in high energy and high-performance activities every day. Even if you increase your time spent by 10 to 30 minutes, you'll feel and see a difference in the success and achievement in your life.

2. Success in Relationships

It's not just work or tasks that are affected by this refocused definition. The definition of **Success = High Energy + High Performance** applies to relationships too.

Think of a person you have a great relationship with. You really enjoy being around them. Time flies by when you are together, and you feel inspired to be a better person and do or be more after being with that person.

- How is your "performance" when you are with them? Are you a good listener? Funny? Open and authentic? Silly? Kind? Attentive? Generous?
- What is your energy like? It doesn't have to be high, frenetic energy but it is usually sustaining, increasing energy rather than draining.

While some people bring out the best in us, the activities you do with that person, the thoughts, feelings, and attitude you have also contribute to your energy and performance in that relationship.

> **Lisa**: I have a friend whom I love to be around. Every time we talk or go for a walk, she asks great

questions to help me reflect. I become more thoughtful about my own life, I listen deeply and feel motivated to be and do more. My friend says our time together has the same effect on her. It is a rich and engaging friendship for both of us.

The definition of success in relationships varies according to the type of relationship and your personal success measures (do you need to feel loved, respected, helpful, etc. in that relationship). However, even relationship success has at least these two ingredients of energy and performance.

So, How Do I Refocus the Pressure to Achieve?

Now that you've explored some nuances of success in tasks and relationships, let's explore your life! Be honest with yourself and take the time to go beneath the surface answers and give yourself a full picture of each activity, arena, and relationship you explore using the questions below. The questions are good. The quality of your insights will come from the quality of your answers - be honest and thorough.

Choose a relationship, situation or arena of your life and redefine success there using the questions below.

Refocusing The Pressure to Achieve:

1) What is my <u>current</u> definition of success in this situation/relationship?

   a) What does it mean to "perform" in this situation?

2) What brings me energy as I create performance?

3) What decreases my energy?

4) What can I do to increase my energy even more?

5) How will I know when I have both energy and performance?

    a) What will I do? How will I feel? What results will I get (in both energy and performance?)

6) What is my insight and next step?

Another Example to Lock It In

Here is an example of how Lisa recently used the questions above to get unstuck in a work situation.

> **Lisa**: In my work, I decided to learn and apply a new-to-me organic social media marketing strategy to promote a new training course I was launching. I hadn't had any experience using social media to generate leads for a business product. This was all new to me. I bought a training program and coach to help me learn how. I had gone through all the training and now it was time to apply it...and I dreaded it. I kept putting off the marketing work I knew I needed to do.
>
> I don't like trying to connect with strangers through social media. It feels fake and manipulative. I feel like I'm putting personal things out there and it's very uncomfortable not knowing how those things will be received. So, I create more intellectual posts that don't feel connective or authentic. It just feels "yucky" to me. I procrastinate, and I don't do it. As a result, my business doesn't grow, and I don't meet new people. I know I **should**, I just really don't want to!
>
> Here is how I used the coaching questions to get "unstuck".

1. *What is my personal performance measure in this situation?*
   a. *What does it mean to "perform" in this situation?* "Make contacts and sales every day" is the goal from my marketing coach but it feels too big, scary and overwhelming in an arena I already feel uncomfortable in. So, I procrastinate. My new goal is to spend 60 minutes a day connecting with people and offering value online. THAT I feel I can do, and it taps into the "why" I'm doing this anyway...to offer value to people I wouldn't otherwise be able to reach.
2. *What brings me energy as I create performance?* The parts I like are offering comments to people on their posts and once I get into it, the writing of posts that explain people's problems and how I can help is fun...it starts to flow. When I start by connecting with others first, then writing my own posts isn't as hard.
3. *What decreases my energy?* Thinking about social media marketing and focusing on the pressure I feel to earn a certain dollar amount from it. And, thinking about trying to connect with hundreds of invisible strangers whom I don't know and who don't know me feels overwhelming and scary.
4. *What can I do to increase my energy even more?* Focus on the people I am trying to help - they are out there looking for what I know. I can connect and help them. Don't focus on the "success" of a sale. Focus on the success of connecting and finding people who are

looking for the help I offer. That feels energizing to me.

5. **How will I know when I have both energy and performance?**
   a. **What will I do? How will I feel? What results will I get (in both energy and performance?)** Sales will come. I'll feel proud of myself for working one hour a day on it and time will fly by. It will become a habit. I'll get better at it and will have more fun. I'll stop fighting myself to "make" myself do it. I'll do it as a matter of habit and will start to enjoy it too.

6. **What is my insight and next step?** Insight: When I focus on helping, it is easier to step out of my comfort zone and write posts and invite people into conversations. When I focus on selling, I get scared, and writing gets hard. Next Step: I just created a little reminder note and put it on my computer. It says, "They are looking for my solution. They feel stuck and uncertain. I can help. Social media helps them find me and me find them. Go connect! Help someone today!" I am going to read that every day before I start my 60 minutes of social media marketing. And I've scheduled my "outreach" time for the mornings when I have the most energy.

What do you notice in that story that seems relevant to you? Write down your thoughts.

If you haven't already done so, use the coaching questions above to explore an arena, relationship or situation where you feel stuck. Answer each question fully and then come back to the next section below. Take a few minutes and do it now.

Conclusion

If you want more success in your life, and less overwhelming pressure, start Refocusing the Pressure to Achieve by expanding your definition of success. Make sure it includes the critical ingredients of both energy and performance. Then, explore what brings energy and performance for you in the situations and relationships of your life. If you want more success, you've got to know what it looks like, so you know if you have achieved it or not. And knowing what it looks like means figuring out what is bringing you energy and what is draining energy; what is the performance standard you are trying to reach and is it a good standard?

This new definition of success applies to both tasks and relationships. By applying the coaching questions in this section, you'll learn to recognize when you aren't where you want to be and then you can employ your new strategies to recover and get back to where you do want to be. By Refocusing the Pressure to Achieve on your new definition of success, you'll create both energy and performance.

The better you get at recognizing when you are off track and the quicker that you get back on track, the more time you'll spend in high energy and performance, the more success you'll create in your life!

Self-Coaching Steps to Help You Get Unstuck

Refocusing the Pressure to Achieve:

1) What is my <u>current</u> definition of success in this situation/relationship?
    a) What does it mean to "perform" in this situation?
2) What brings me energy as I create performance?
3) What decreases my energy?
4) What can I do to increase my energy even more?
5) How will I know when I have both energy and performance?
    a) What will I do? How will I feel? What results will I get (in both energy and performance?)
6) What is my insight and next step?

For more resources for Refocusing the Pressure to Achieve, check out www.StuckNoMoreBook.com/Resources using the QR Code below.

CHAPTER 5

Listen to Me!

"How well we communicate is not determined by how well we say things but how well we are understood [and understand others]." – Andrew Grove, Intel CEO

"I just want you to listen to me!"

Even at the best of times, communication can be tough. When relationships are strong, communication feels easy. Yet when they aren't working, it can seem impossible to communicate, leaving us feeling disconnected, frustrated, and exhausted. Unfortunately, it is often the case that the more disconnection there is between people, the harder it is to communicate, which in turn increases the disconnection!

If you are thinking...

- "It's like we're living on different planets now. We used to talk and laugh about everything, but now, even saying 'hi' can start a war. Why can't we just get along like before?"

- "I try so hard to make you understand what I'm feeling, but it's like talking to a brick wall. It feels like you don't even care. Do I mean anything to you at all?"

- "Every time I try to explain how I feel, it's like I'm just making things worse. I'm so tired of this. Why can't anything I say come out right?"
- "I'm doing everything I can to fix this, but it feels like I'm the only one who cares. It's just not fair. Don't you see how hard I'm trying?"
- "I've tried everything to make us understand each other better, but nothing's working. It's like we're cursed to keep getting it wrong. Is there even a point in trying anymore?"

Or if you are feeling…

- Frustrated and exhausted from repeated failed attempts to communicate effectively
- Lonely or disconnected because there is a lack of understanding or empathy from the other person
- Confused about why communication that once was easy and effective has become difficult
- Resentment or irritation because you're the only one trying to address the communication issues
- Helplessness or resignation, wondering if the situation can ever improve or if it's worth the effort to try…

Then, the **Reducing Communication Noise** tool will help you to…

- See the situation for what it really is.
- Try a different approach.
- Feel that you are hearing and being heard.

Maybe there is a voice in your head right now saying, "I already tried everything. It's impossible to change. I can't change them, and they won't change!"

Even if you think that you have 'tried everything', there is still hope. You will be able to find answers to the questions you have, ONLY after you see the situation for what it really is and try a different approach. This chapter will help you do just that, and given that you are still reading, it's probably safe to assume you are willing to try, even just one more time.

What Are the Self-Coaching Questions to Help You Get Unstuck?

Reducing Communication Noise:

1) What is happening in the communication?
    a) What external noise is present?
    b) What internal noise is present for me?
    c) What internal noise might be present for them?
2) What are they trying to communicate? and What is important about this to them?
3) How can I confirm my understanding of what they are saying?

What Does This Tool Really Mean and How/Why Does it Work?

This tool is all about paying attention to the things you can control inside the relationship and in your communication with others. By focusing your attention on these things, you can transform your frustration. You will be Stuck No More.

To understand this tool and how it works, let's first explore what people often think is happening in communication, what is really happening, and what to do about it.

Communication Basics – An Oversimplified Model

Understanding how communication happens is the first step to recognizing when it is effective, and when it isn't.

Communication should be simple - I talk, you listen. Or perhaps the other way round. You talk, I listen. At its core, people describe communication as requiring only 3 things: a sender, a receiver, and a message.

As a sender, I have a message that I want the receiver to hear. I send it, they receive it. Then, if we are in a conversation, we swap roles, and the other person sends the message they want me to hear, and I receive it. Simple. You may have even learned this in elementary/primary school.

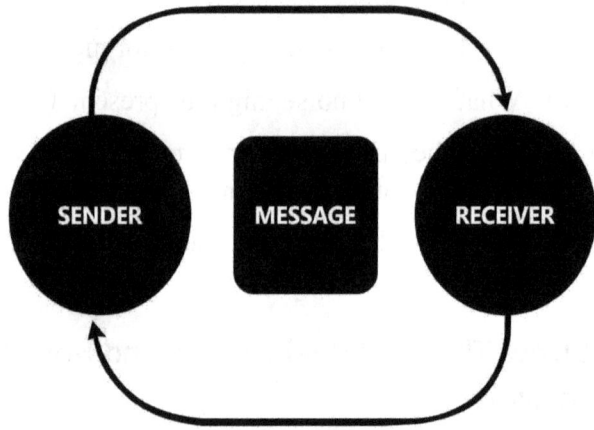

Simple? Perhaps. Easy? Not often. Experience tells us that communication doesn't work like this. How do we know? Because sometimes it is difficult.

Sometimes the others' message doesn't make sense. Other times they just can't seem to understand even the simplest of concepts that we think we are sharing with great clarity.

Take a moment and remember a time when someone didn't understand what you were saying, when they just couldn't (or wouldn't) get it. What did you do?

If you are like most people, you would have considered a different way to share the message. You may have clarified your message, removed ambiguity, or found a simple and straightforward way to articulate the core of your message. Yet, even with all of this simplification, the other person still may have missed your point and misunderstood your message.

In this oversimplified model there are only 3 things that could go wrong and cause communication to break down:

1) **Message**: The message itself might not be clear.

2) **Sender**: How we send the message might be ineffective.

3) **Receiver**: The receiver cannot/will not receive the message clearly.

If there are three things that could go wrong, then when something does go wrong, we respond by changing one or more of these three things.

It often looks kind of like this:

> When communication breaks down or feels difficult, we find another way to share our message. We use different words, give more context, clearly spell out any connections and simplify our message as much as possible. When this still doesn't work, then we try to clarify how the message is sent. WE SPEAK LOUDER, we emphasize key words or E-NUN-CI-ATE more. Sometimes ... We ... Slow ... Down ... How ... We ... Talk. ... Speaking ... The ... Message ... One ... Word ... At ... A ... Time.

> Surely if they can understand each word, then they can understand the simplified message I am trying to send!

After we have taken these steps, things feel pretty clear. If there are three things that can go wrong with communication and we have clarified our message, and sent it in simple and clear words, there is only one thing left.

"If I have fixed the other two things, it must mean that they are the problem! They are just not listening to me!!"

When we have tried everything we can, and the problem lies with them, then we are stuck, because **"There is nothing else I can do!"** We feel helpless and become trapped, blaming the other person. And we give up trying to communicate.

This is a very common scenario. You may have seen it play out in front of your eyes in meetings at work. Or perhaps it is an everyday occurrence as you watch kids communicate - or try to!

The problem in this scenario is that the model is incomplete and oversimplified. It is very possible that the other person is actually listening to you! But, because there are more steps and influences in communication, something else could be getting in the way ... something that may have more to do with you than with them.

While we never like to see ourselves as the problem, this is actually a good thing, because it means that you can change things. You can get the conversation unstuck!

Communication Basics - What is Really Going On

Unlike the super simple model shown earlier, here is how communication actually works. And why it can feel so difficult to get right, especially when the relationship is strained or there has been miscommunication in the past.

As we share the expanded model next, don't feel like you need to remember all of the steps and influences. Just recognize that communication is more complex than Message, Send and Receive. This means that there are more actions you can take to positively influence successful communication. There is hope!

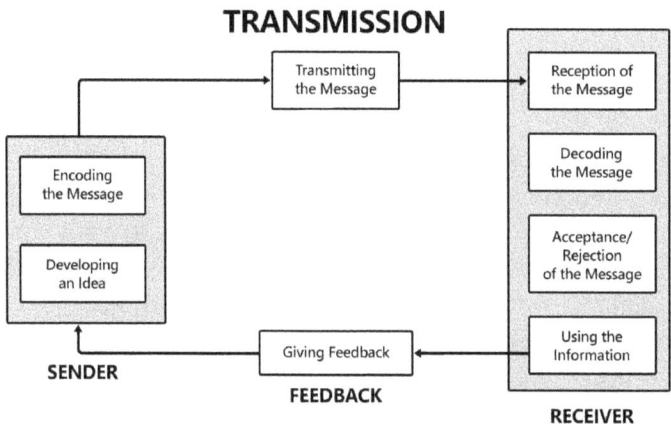

You can see the three basic components of communication are still here - the message, sending and receiving. But as you can see, the sender and receiver are actually doing multiple things at once.

The Sender

As the sender, we must first develop what we want to communicate. This involves identifying our intention, and the message we want to be received. We have to figure out **what** to communicate, **why** we want to communicate, as well as **how** to structure our message and then we need to actually transmit the message (i.e. to speak or send the email, etc.). This message needs to be sent within the context and environment in which we find ourselves, choosing volume, tone and pace, as well as the type of words that will be understood by our audience. As we saw in the Changing Your Internal Story chapter, each of these steps is crafted in response to how we have interpreted what is happening (story), as well as what we are trying to achieve (purpose).

The Receiver

Now put yourself in the shoes of the person receiving the message. From this side, to receive a message, we must physically receive (hear) the message, and then interpret the literal and emotional meaning by making sense of the words, tone, body language and try to determine the intent of the sender (i.e. work out the message that we think they wanted us to hear). Now that we have crafted some interpretation (story), we must decide whether we accept or reject some, or all parts of the message, figure out what to do with the information and feelings conveyed in the message, as well as our own in response, and then decide if we want to reply.

If we choose to reply, then we need to determine what message we want to send, how to structure it, how to send it, and then we need to send it. All of this, of course, is happening from within, and influenced by, the story that we created in response to their message, and what we think it is telling us, both directly and indirectly, and the purpose of their message. Now that we have our response, we share our own message in response – we now become the sender.

As we send this message, in response to the one we received, we automatically convey information as to whether or not we received the initially intended message, as well as other information that we send.

It's complex!

The Complexity

While there are many steps and a lot to do, most of the time we move through each step unconsciously. We have practiced these steps so many times in our lives that we don't need to stop and think about each one. They are habitual and automated, and we usually deal with them unconsciously. It is especially easy in simple conversations, within trusting relationships, where all these components can happen very quickly. That is where these habits often work well.

However, our unconscious communication habits often fail us when the situation is complex, uncertain, surprising or when we are emotionally elevated.

When it works, unconsciousness is great, as it saves having to think about each step. However, when it isn't working, there is great power in expanding your awareness. Building this awareness allows you to notice what is happening, what is working and what needs to be addressed.

> **Something To Think About**
>
> As adults, we are often patient and flexible when communicating with children, because we know they are still learning how to best express themselves. We do this, not just because of their skill level, but also with compassion for what is happening for them emotionally and mentally. We strive to understand their perspective with empathy and attentiveness.
>
> Yet, when talking to adults, we often forget that not everyone's the same. People come from different backgrounds, have different feelings, and face different challenges that can make communicating difficult. So, it's really important to be just as patient and understanding with other grown-ups as we are with children. This means being open to the fact that there's a lot more going on when someone's trying to communicate than just the words they're using.

> Being more understanding and kind in your conversations can help avoid misunderstandings and make everyone feel more connected and respected.

To make matters worse, there are usually multiple layers of noise present on top of all of these steps. Sometimes this noise is quiet, sometimes so loud that the messages get lost, corrupted, or misinterpreted. This is especially true in complex situations, with complex messages and complex relationships, where noise can derail communication very quickly. For most of us, every day is an example of complex situations!

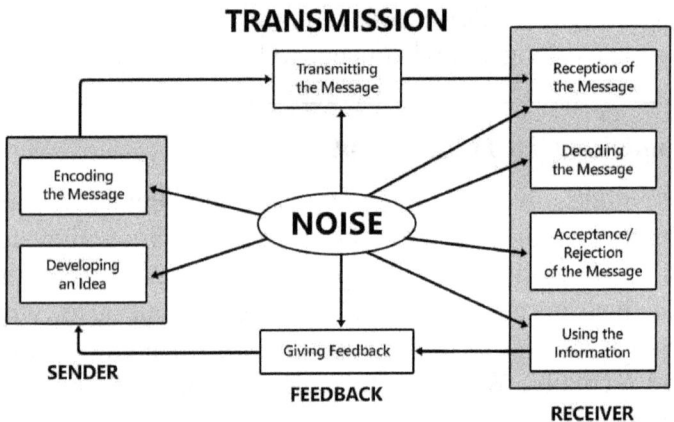

Noise

Noise can be a lot of things. It can be external or internal.

External noise can be actual external noise in the environment. For example, the middle of the dance floor at a loud concert is probably not the best place to have a deep and meaningful conversation about an important topic. Trying to shout over the deafening music in the middle of a gyrating and dancing crowd could be very distracting (at best). We are all familiar with this kind of external noise.

In addition to the physical environmental noise of a concert (or sporting event, busy subway, crowded restaurant, etc.), noise can also be situational. For example, if you are in the middle of a job interview, this is not the time that you want to listen to your kids' story about finger painting. When your favorite sporting team is about to score, you are not likely to want to have a conversation about your neighbor's birthday party.

Context and the situation are also essential to create relevance for messages, and without relevance our listening is distracted, focused elsewhere or we are just not open to receiving.

Thankfully, external noise is often quite simple to identify and control, and is often addressed by choosing a suitable environment for the conversation. This can be as simple as booking a time, closing the door to the office, turning off the television, or putting down your phone.

More often, however, noise is internal.

Internal noise lies inside you or within the other person. It includes any thought, feeling or expectation that gets in the way of receiving a message. Because it is not as obvious as external noise, it is much more subtly distracting than external noise, and therefore "louder" in that it can have a larger effect on disturbing communication.

Think for a moment about what sort of internal noise gets in the way of you intently listening to another person.

While the words may be different, most people answer with things like:

> feeling hungry; being busy; the temperature; the score on the television; the message that just arrived on your phone; the email you haven't replied to; what is happening around you; the tightness of your belt; addictions; boredom; past relationships; situations that you are reminded of; your

mindset/motivation; tasks you need to get done; what you expect from the other person; what you are expecting the person to say (or how they say it); expectations about yourself; goals and objectives you might have; the story you are telling yourself about the other person, yourself or the situation; your intentions; judgements ... and more, much more.

All of these are examples of noise because they can interfere with your ability to effectively send and receive messages. They compete for your attention and therefore reduce your ability to be present to what is happening in the conversation. Sometimes this noise can be present and not negatively impact communication, other times you will miss essential details. The danger with noise, is not only that you miss details, but that you may not be aware that you have missed them! You think that you have received the whole message, when in fact, you have missed critical parts and are not even aware of it!

Often, we don't notice that this internal noise is present. Other times, we realize that it is present, but do not see it as noise. Interestingly, when we are busy thinking our own thoughts, we often view others and what they are trying to communicate **as the noise**!

Examples of Internal and External Noise

Sender and Receiver Internal	Situational/Contextual External
Distracting or negative thoughts Intense feelings Open or closed mindset Expectations and assumptions Judgements Lack of purpose Internal stories about myself or others My interpretation of your reaction or anticipation of your reaction Fatigue, hunger, stress, physical discomfort Time constraints Waiting for something	Music and Sounds Televisions and Phones Tasks and activities Other conversations in the area Audience Visual distractions Weather Temperature Location distractions Unsuitable Location Unsuitable Situation

See more details and examples at
www.StuckNoMoreBook.com/Resources.

When you take a moment to think about it, the solution is often very clear. Where there is noise that is getting in the way of effective communication, reduce the noise. If the music is on, turn it down. If you are thinking about your tasks and to-do list, stop and listen. If someone isn't ready to listen (involved in another project), wait.

In many ways, clarity of PURPOSE is essential as it helps us decide what is important, and what is noise. Simply taking a moment to answer the question **"what is important here?"** will help clarify purpose and identify different types of noise. When you are aware of internal and external noise, you can choose where to focus, what to listen to, what to address, and what to ignore. It can also help you decide the best way to send the message.

This, however, is often more easily said than done, because our internal noise is amplified when we are frustrated, stressed, busy or upset. In these situations, responses are driven by habitual behaviors of defensiveness, justification, and judgement. These feelings and responses get louder when you feel, "THEY are not listening to me!".

Lisa: Early on in our marriage, when I wanted to say something to my husband, Joe, I would just start speaking. If he was busy, I would tell him what he needed to know or ask the question that was most important to me at that moment. Unfortunately, this led to quite a lot of frustration as he didn't listen, asked frustrating questions, or gave answers that were completely irrelevant to what I had asked. It wasn't long before I realized that perhaps he wasn't quite ready for the conversation. By ambushing him with my communication, I was setting myself up for failure.

To me, his hobby stuff or activities were noise when I was trying to share something important with him. Clearly, whatever he was doing at that moment was not nearly as important as what I wanted to talk about. (Right?!)

To him, my communication was noise that was disruptive to the task he was involved in, which is why, to him, it felt like I was interrupting.

Since those early days, Joe has helped me to check to see if he is ready to listen to what I have to say

BEFORE I start talking. I now look for what might be internal and external noise for him BEFORE I start communicating.

I remind myself that just because I am ready for the conversation doesn't mean he is also ready. So, I say to him, "I'd like to talk with you about *a subject*. Is now a good time? If not, when would work best?"

Sometimes he stops what he is doing, and we talk right then and there. At other times he gives me a timeframe that will allow him to finish what he is doing so he can focus on the conversation. The important thing is; by checking in first, I help to reduce the internal and external noise around us both. This gives us a fighting chance at better communication. And when I forget to do it, Joe reminds me by saying, "I'm in the middle of something. Can you give me 10 minutes?" Being intentional about reducing noise has really helped our communication.

As we saw at the beginning of the chapter, it is very easy to go straight to judgement and blame the other person (or people) for not listening, or not communicating effectively. While there may be some truth in it, that story leaves you powerless to change the situation. Instead, pay attention and become aware of the noise within yourself, as well as the noise that you may be contributing to the other person.

Remember, as we are feeling unheard, we tend to amplify or adjust our message. Others do the same. In many cases, when we are feeling unheard, so are they. As we feel disconnected from them, they feel disconnected from us. This leads us both to behave in ways that can increase the noise for both of us and messes up the communication.

Rather than giving up and blaming, you can get unstuck by overcoming the noise.

Overcoming Your Noise

The first step to more effective communication is to implement a simple strategy to minimize your own noise, allowing you to better focus on hearing the other person.

Many people question this statement. Let's say it again:

The first step to more effective communication is for you to focus and hear the other person.

This might initially seem counterproductive, but it is key. If you want others to hear more of what you are saying, the first step is to hear more of what they are saying. This helps to rebuild the connection between the two of you while reducing noise that they might experience if they aren't feeling heard.

Specifically, your aim here is to build connection by seeking to understand what they are trying to say. Not what it might mean for you, and not whether you agree or not. Simply to understand what they are trying to say.

This step takes the simple communication model shown earlier and uses it to your advantage. Firstly, step into the receiver mode. It is very difficult to evolve a challenging conversation as the sender, throwing more ideas at them will not increase their readiness to listen. Instead, slow down, and meet them where they are. Make sure that you are hearing what they are sending, then they can become more ready to receive as you gently communicate back. Effective communication is about giving and receiving, if they are not yet ready to receive, then you take charge and receive what they are giving. This is how you can quickly change the relational dynamics, from the role of receiver.

> **Something To Think About**
>
> Typically, people think they can change the communication dynamic best when they are in the role of sender. Initially this makes sense. If we are going to do something differently, then someone needs to do something differently, so I can do it. We take the initiative and take action - as a sender.
>
> However, think about all the parental lectures you received as a teenager. Did any of them actually improve communication?
>
> While taking initiative as the sender feels like something we can control, it is like trying to walk through a closed door. It actually doesn't matter how elegantly you walk; you won't get in! This belief is based on the incorrect assumption that sending is active, and receiving is passive. This is far from the truth.
>
> Now, think about a time when someone deeply listened to you and really tried to understand your point of view before sharing anything back. What was the impact? Exactly!
>
> You have more power to change the dynamic from the role of receiver than sender. And yet, most of us try to change things from the role of sender. So, the secret is to take action, not by sending, but by receiving. Get really good at receiving and see what a difference it makes.

As a receiver, you have the power to radically increase how effective the communication is, by intentionally receiving the message of the other person. To do this, you focus on receiving and understanding the message being sent.

As you focus your attention on understanding the message, you cut through the internal and external noise. It is important to slow down the process and focus only on receiving and understanding the message that the other person is trying to send.

An easy way to slow down the process and step into receiver mode is to get curious. It is important to add curiosity to your listening, as without it, we think we know what will be said – so we stop listening. Yes, thinking you know what they are saying is a form of noise. When you lean in with curiosity and think, "I wonder what they are trying to communicate?" and "What is important about this to them?" rather than, "What am I going to say?" you open yourself up to hearing the intent of the sender, not just what you were expecting.

Getting curious helps to reduce your own internal noise so you can be even more curious and truly hear the other person. Put down the phone, turn away from your computer, make eye contact, stop thinking of other things and just be curious, focused and present. It will make understanding their intent and meaning much faster!

The Reducing Communication Noise tool will help you overcome the noise and clarify your understanding of the other person's message. Once the other person feels more understood and heard, they will be more open to receiving your message. This is how you can take responsibility to transform your communication and feel more listened to.

So, How Do I Reduce Communication Noise?

Here are the questions to ask and answer for yourself when you are stuck in communication, feel that you aren't being heard and are unable to see how to get unstuck. These questions are the initial questions to ask, but keep digging and asking yourself follow-up questions until you quiet the noise for yourself and really see and hear what is happening in the communication between yourself and the other person.

Self-Coaching Steps to Help You Get Unstuck

Reducing Communication Noise:

1) What is happening in the communication?

    a) What external noise is present for us?

    Reduce or remove external things that attract attention, i.e. Music, phones, tasks.

    b) What internal noise is present for me?

    Focus on the other person. Stop thinking of other things. Put down your phone. Focus your attention on them. Make eye contact. Get curious.

    c) What internal noise might be present for them?

    What might they be thinking or feeling that could be a distraction?

2) What are they trying to communicate? and What is important about this to them?

    Let go of the responsibility to respond to what they are saying and get curious first about their message.

3) How can I confirm my understanding of what they are saying?

    Show that you are listening and focusing on them.

    Focus on understanding and checking your understanding of the sender's intent. Do they think you understand?

A Metaphor to Lock It In

A conversation is like playing catch. It involves us having a ball (a message), and then we throw the ball (sending the message) to the other person who catches (receives) it. It requires both of us to be focused on each other and not distracted (noise).

Let's think about what helps us play catch.

If I want to play catch with you, there is no point throwing the ball to you when you are busy with another task - this will cause frustration, and possibly even damage or injury. Before throwing the ball, it makes sense that we are in an area that is safe for ball throwing, and that you are ready to play.

How should I throw the ball? hard? soft? Ultimately, if I want you to catch the ball, I should throw it to you at a speed and in a way that makes it easy for you to catch. I should throw it how you want to catch it, not only how I want it thrown.

It would also be a poor decision for me to throw one ball at you, pick up another and throw it, then grab and throw a third before I'm sure you've caught the first ball. With all of these balls flying towards them, the other person will likely be overwhelmed, distracted, rushed and have to defend against missiles flying towards their face.

When picturing a game of catch, it becomes easy to see that the environment makes a difference. We want an environment that allows us both to concentrate on the balls, and to work together to throw them back and forth. We remove distractions, we create space, and we help each other out.

Unfortunately, these are all things we often forget to do in 'conversation' as we send messages to the people around us. We ask questions or share important information before we have their full attention; burst out of nowhere with pointed and emotive questions; rapid firing questions or pile multiple topics on top of each other and do all of this in an environment filled with noise and distractions.

Just like a great game of catch, the secret to effective communication is to first get the other person's attention, ensure they are ready to catch. You can then find the right environment that allows you both to focus on the game, and only then start to gently toss balls. Send your message so they can catch it and pay particular attention to how they are 'throwing' the messages so you can catch them with curiosity and compassion.

Conclusion

Now that you are informed, motivated and hopeful that things can change in communication, we feel obligated to share that this tool doesn't work all of the time. Some of the things we've talked about in other chapters can still get in the way of good communication.

For example, if you come from a place of self or "other" judgment, communication doesn't usually get better. If you operate from a story that says the other person won't listen, change will be slow. If you and your communication partner aren't aligned on purpose, communication will stay bumpy. And, if there is mental or physical illness that is playing into the situation, that noise may be too loud to overcome.

So, manage yourself. Apply what you have learned in the other chapters. Get curious. And apply what you've learned here. In most situations, you'll be surprised at the change in yourself and in others' reactions to you. It's worth a try because…

With Practice, It Can Work Wonders!

The hardest communication situation in your life CAN get better. As you've been reading this chapter, you've been thinking about the most frustrating communication situation and person in your life. And we invite you to start practicing what you have learned here with an "easy" relationship. Practice a little there, get some confidence and then apply your new skills with the hard communication partner.

Self-Coaching Steps to Help You Get Unstuck

Reducing Communication Noise:

1) What is happening in the communication?
    a) What external noise is present?
    b) What internal noise is present for me?
    c) What internal noise might be present for them?
2) What are they trying to communicate? and What is important about this to them?
3) How can I confirm my understanding of what they are saying?

For more communication resources from Reducing Communication Noise and bonus materials around communication styles, check out www.StuckNoMoreBook.com/Resources using the QR Code below.

Listen to Me!

CHAPTER 6

What to Do Next

"Knowledge isn't power. Applied knowledge is Power." - Eric Thomas

What To Do Next

We are firm believers in learning and then practicing what you've learned. Through this book, you've learned new things and been reminded of things you've forgotten or don't apply consistently.

Now, it's time to apply what you've learned, over and over, so that you learn to coach yourself, naturally and effectively, through most of the places, relationships, and situations where you get stuck in your everyday life.

The high-level questions on the next page will help you determine which strategy to try first, to get yourself unstuck from your everyday problem. If you can't clearly answer these questions for the situation or relationship where you feel stuck, then go to the chapter indicated and use that tool to get unstuck.

What to Do Next

What Are the Self-Coaching Questions to Help You Get Unstuck?

Determining Which Strategy/Self-Coaching Questions Can Help Me Best in This Situation

1) **What is my purpose?** And, what do I want in this situation/relationship? *Chapter 2*

2) **What story am I telling myself about what is happening?** How does that story serve me or hurt me? What is a better story that could be true and serve me? *Chapter 3*

3) **How would I rate my achievement, my energy and performance, in this situation/relationship?** What do I want to change about energy and/or performance? *Chapter 4*

4) **What external and internal noise is present when I am communicating?** What do they need from me to show I have heard their message? How can I share my message to help them receive it clearly? *Chapter 5*

How Do I Do It?

Notice that you are becoming more aware of your own internal voice - what it is saying and how to ask yourself questions to get better answers.

As promised, this book hasn't solved 100% of your problems, but it has given you self-coaching guides. Now you can find your own way out of 80% of the everyday problems that stress you and make you feel stuck in the not knowing and the not doing.

For those situations where you are still stuck, there are more resources and of course, we are big fans of hiring a coach to help you find your own answers through great questions (and sometimes a little guidance). We've added some of our favorite additional resources at the end of the book, but first, we have a word of caution for you.

What you need most NOW is to APPLY what you have learned in this book, not to search out more tools.

First, practice using the questions and ideas in this book as tools.

Practice asking yourself better questions.

Practice being honest with yourself - with confidence that you'll find the answers and with a little vulnerability knowing that you can't see everything without a little help.

Practice getting unstuck.

Practice now.

You can do it.

What to Do Next

Some of our favorite additional resources at the end of this book so that we have a word of caution for you as well.

What you need right NOW is to FUEL up what you have learned in this book, not to search out more tools.

First, practice using the questions and ideas in this book as tools.

Practice, practice, practice! No exceptions.

The best books in the world are of no use if they sit on the shelf and not read, used and with more tools as well knowing when to use and when not to use the ones available.

Additional Resources

"A little knowledge that acts is worth infinitely more than much knowledge that is idle." – **Kahlil Gibran**

Please first master what you have learned in this book - these self-coaching questions. Join our private Facebook Group "Stuck No More People" to hear and share stories, questions, challenges and solutions to getting unstuck.

https://www.facebook.com/groups/stucknomorepeople

Also, download the additional resources that accompany this book at www.stucknomorebook.com/resources or by using the QR code below.

Additional Resources

Additional Resources

You can also download a Group Discussion Guide with discussion questions for groups, teams and families to discuss the tools in the book.

You can find that Discussion Guide at *www.stucknomorebook.com/discussion* or by using the QR Code below.

Group Discussion Guide

If you still find yourself ready to learn and practice more strategies, below is a list of some of our favorite resources to learn to self-coach and find better solutions for your life.

Assessments

Strengths Multiplier Assessment by Thrivin. Determine your natural strengths, ways of being, doing, thinking, and evaluating yourself and others. www.thrivin.global

Books/Chapters

The Success Principles by Jack Canfield - Inner Critic to Inner Coach Chapter. Explore your larger purpose in life, not just situational purpose.

Live Life in Crescendo by Stephen R Covey and Cynthia Covey Haller. How do you take your life to the next level and make an impact, at any age, anywhere?

Shift Up: Strengths Strategies for Optimal Living by DeAnna Murphy, Lisa C. Gregory, Steve Jeffs. Utilize your unique strengths to create optimal energy and performance in life and work.

Man's Search for Meaning by Victor E. Frankl. Identify a purpose to your life through one of three ways: the completion of tasks, caring for another person, or finding meaning by facing suffering with dignity.

Online Learning

Self-Leadership by People Acuity. Learn how to create your own conditions for bringing your very best self every single day and influence others to do the same. www.thrivin.global

One on One Coaching

For Executives and Senior Organizational Leaders, Personal Coaching or Coaching of Middle Manager, Frontline Leaders or Individual Contributors, contact Lisa and Steve at info@stucknomorebook.com

Group/Organizational Coaching with Assessments

For corporate engagements, contact Lisa and Steve at info@stucknomorebook.com

Keynote or Conference Appearances

To have Lisa and/or Steve speak at your next event, contact our team at www.stucknomorebook.com or by emailing info@stucknomorebook.com

Additional Resources

www.ingramcontent.com/pod-product-compliance
Lightning Source LLC
Chambersburg PA
CBHW060514030426
42337CB00015B/1884